HAUNTED FLORIDA
LOVE STORIES

CHRISTOPHER BALZANO

Haunted America

Published by Haunted America
A Division of The History Press
Charleston, SC
www.historypress.com

All photos are from the author's collection unless otherwise noted.

First published 2020

Manufactured in the United States

ISBN 9781467145688

Library of Congress Control Number: 2020938644

Notice: The information in this book is true and complete to the best of our knowledge. It is offered without guarantee on the part of the author or The History Press. The author and The History Press disclaim all liability in connection with the use of this book.

To Natalie Crist, my inspiration, my navigator and the little voice whispering to me throughout the writing of this book. Without your empathy, passion, intelligence, humor and outlook, these stories would remain untold, and I would be left wondering what it is all about.

CONTENTS

PREFACE

Years ago, deep into my career as a paranormal writer and investigator, Tim Weisberg of the radio show *Spooky Southcoast* referred to me as an analytical folklorist. I liked the title because it sounded important and made me feel like there was something that I was doing in the field that might be different from other people. I had started my journey documenting the hauntings and legends at my college dormitory at Emerson College, the famously haunted Charlesgate Hotel, and made a name for myself unlocking the stories associated with the Red Headed Hitchhiker of Route 44 in Rehoboth, Massachusetts. Back then, all I needed was a story, a location and enough gas money to seek out the account—more reporter and storyteller than ghost hunter. Somewhere along the way, I found the need to investigate, and then all bets were off. The "heart of the haunting," as I called it, took a backseat to trying to prove that the locations I went to were haunted.

Then I moved to Florida in 2008. I felt called back to the tales of ghosts I had been hearing for years and not the technology that had entered the field. I put the whole thing down and continued with my life as a teacher. But these stories have a way of calling you back.

I began *Tripping on Legends* with my cohost and fellow storyteller, Natalie Crist, on Halloween 2016. I had read about the Venice Bus Depot in Kim Cool's book and wanted to experience the ghost Ringling train for myself. No equipment and no data collecting—just two curious minds, a few two-dollar bills and a foggy night. It's what's called "legend tripping," an activity that goes back generations, though it now has a negative connotation in the paranormal community. We have always stayed true to our original purpose:

> *Let's take a trip.*
> *Small town, USA. This is where the pulse of the paranormal resides. There are thousands of stories and experiences out there. Some have been told and retold hundreds of times, and some are kept hidden, known only by the people that live there. This is where we come in. We're exploring the untold and breaking down the overly familiar. Journeying through the one stoplight towns and discovering local urban legends, myths, lore, and paranormal episodes. Researching the backgrounds and developing the voices unheard. Our goal is not to capture evidence, but rather to capture the moment and bring our listeners along for the ride.*

I have spent the last three years legend tripping any ghost story I could find in the state of Florida with only these conditions to it: there has to be a backstory as interesting as the haunting itself; the haunting has to be something people have talked about for years; and it has to reflect the town in which it takes place, the time it was created or say something about the people who spread it. During these three years, as well as the other twenty I spent doing research in New England, one theme keeps coming up again and again: love.

When something unexplained happens, people feel the need to explain it. It's our nature. We run it through what we know and what is closest to us and come up with something we can wrap our minds around. There is a light in the sky. A ufologist will tell you it is a UFO. Someone with a deep religious background might tell you it's an angel. Someone interested in ghosts will say you have just seen a spirit.

The same can be said about the *why* of the unknown. Why does this glowing figure walk along this stretch of road in my town? When we don't know, we fall back on what we know the most, and a good love story, even when tragic, is always on our minds. Love is passion, and we can imagine that desire living beyond our death in the same way we can imagine tragedy causing a spirit to stay. These stories are familiar, and in the face of something as spooky and unsettling as a ghost, there is a certain level of understanding and comfort we get from attaching a love story to it. *Romeo and Juliet* plays out on every dark road, creepy cemetery and lonely lighthouse we know because we understand the story. Boy meets girl, boy falls in love with girl, bad things happen. It makes sense that there would be a ghost.

There are three basic forms of love covered in these ghostly legends: romantic love, love of family and a passion for your job or something you did in life. They are not organized under headings because so much of the folklore crosses boundaries and getting the story straight is never simple. One person says the bridge is home to a couple who committed suicide together, while another says it's a father looking for his lost son. You can't judge folklore on whether it is true—only if the people who tell it believe it to be so.

Read this book differently than you may other ghost books. There are very few firsthand accounts or substantiation of the tales I am passing on to you. I am not trying to prove that something has happened at these locations or offer you evidence that they are haunted. I'm not even trying to convince you that the legends are true. The best I can do is give you the context and let you decide for yourself. I have been to almost every one of these locations. I have called out, "Mini-Lights, Mini-Lights, come out tonight" and offered up a love potion at Arbuckle Creek. I have waited at Safety Harbor in the rain for a shaman, watched the Manatee River and listened for its song and tried to have conversations with invisible mothers, talking statues and deceased law enforcement officers. The one thing I can tell you is that in the dark, with the history and backstories of these people bouncing around in your brain, whether they are true or not doesn't matter a bit. You can just experience the moment and sense the situation of the legend and understand why people believe.

These legends are validation over verification. I guess that makes them a perfect fit for a love story.

ACKNOWLEDGEMENTS

There is no way to tell a story without hearing it from other people first, and there have been many voices who have guided me throughout the gathering and retelling of these stories. It all begins with Natalie Crist, the woman who acted as the inspiration and guiding force on the many trips showcased in this book. I would also like to thank Jeff Belanger, who gave me encouragement and an old laptop when I had nothing to write with. As he said, a carpenter needs his tools. Even more than with my other books, my children, Devin and Ella, were important in writing this book. They were my travel companions on some of these adventures and dealt with my questions, edits and stress with humor and great suggestions.

I would like to thank the many writers and researchers who laid the groundwork for many of the stories in the book. Thank you, Mark Muncy, for your encouragement and for allowing me to steal from you every once in a while. Dr. Brandy Stark of *Urban Legends of Pinellas County* helped me ground many of the stories, and Rebecca Genesis contributed to my knowledge of different areas of the country. Thank you to Richie Ferrara and Lee Ehrlich for your information on Charlotte and Lee Counties and Elise Van Cise, Margee Unger and Johnathan Dolce for my introduction into Central Florida folklore. Thank you to Paul Benstine and Paranormal Extreme for information about Ringling School of Art and Design.

Telling folklore often involves hitting up librarians, archivists and authorities. I would like to thank the following people who gave me bits and pieces along the way: Mark Bertolami and Rachel Duke of Florida State

University; Michael D. Johnson of the University of Central Florida; Kelly Larson and Paul Croce of Stetson University; Tim Hollis and Christopher Shaffer of Ringling College of Art and Design; and the many rangers, writers, employees and witnesses who told their versions of stories and allowed me to make them mine.

1

TWO DIFFERENT KINDS OF LOVE
AT FORT DESOTO

Some places don't stand a chance. They have their foundations under dark clouds, and in Florida, those kinds of clouds can appear out of nowhere and signal a torrential downpour. They are places where you look back with the fortune of hindsight and wonder what people were thinking even trying to create something there. You could have told them they were wrong to even think about it, and each moment can be seen as part of a curse leaving its breadcrumbs in history. Even in those places, love finds a way to make itself seen. Even in the darkest sea, a fisherman and a mother can shuffle the way we think.

Fort DeSoto Park in St. Petersburg has just about everything to be considered haunted. The name itself might be cursed, if you believe in that kind of thing. The fort, as well as the nearby county and countless other businesses and attractions in Florida, is named for Hernando DeSoto, a Spanish explorer who made it to Florida in 1539. His primary motivation was to clear land for the Spanish and find potential sources of money, especially gold. While he was not as vicious as his predecessor, Pánfilo de Narváez, his men were not afraid to clash with the natives, and his exploits are directly linked to the decimation of the Tocoboga and Western Timucua tribes. Florida is not always an easy place to balance history, and DeSoto is considered a hero and trailblazer and tyrant. He and other conquistadors not only ravaged the living but also disturbed many of the ceremonial and burial mounds in the process of their exploring.

The main armament at Fort DeSoto in Fort DeSoto Park.

In fact, Fort DeSoto is not the first encampment in that area with that name and not the only one with a haunted history. The town of Brooksville, well known for several of its own ghost stories and dark history, established Fort DeSoto in 1840. Increased tension between Floridians and Native Americans and the Seminole War made it important to secure that part of the state with force. The base, however, failed. The town had built it on limestone, and after it was up and running, they found it impossible to get water from the ground. It was abandoned only a few years later, maybe the first sign of a potential curse.

Another sign more directly related to the destruction of the mounds involves the area leading to Fort DeSoto called Tierra Verde. Once the home to several mounds, they were plowed through when successful businessman Fred Berlanti purchased the land in 1959. Although he was warned that they had discovered relics and should stop building, he told his crews to ignore what they had found and press on. According to *The Tampa Triangle* by Bill Miller, after that, Berlanti's other businesses started to fail. He took a private flight to Miami to try to stop the bleeding, and his plane was mysteriously struck out of the sky. Someone who acted as a witness reported that a blue light rose from a lake like a hand, held the plane frozen in the air and then broke it apart, "like a cheap Christmas ornament."

Matters were not better for the fort itself. It was the military outpost that could never seem to get it right. During the Civil War, it was suggested as a place of defense for the Confederacy, who dumped the idea. In 1890, a new Fort DeSoto was established on the coast to defend Tampa Bay against attacks. Even during its construction, there were issues, as the state-of-the-art design met with technical problems and then had to replace the planned concrete with shells during construction because of delays. These shells were most likely discarded remnants of the mounds the original settlers found, like building the disturbed sacred ground right into the structure.

To the south, Egmont Key, another paranormal hot spot and the birthplace of many of the legends of the coast via its lighthouse keeper, was the primary fortification, with DeSoto acting as a backup during the Spanish-American War. It was the little brother who was constantly being made fun of and never saw any action. It fired its guns only in practice but never in battle, and the people who were forced to serve there had to deal with diseases like yellow fever, intense heat and humidity, insects and the idea that they were probably not going to see much action. When one health commissioner sent a letter detailing the horrors at DeSoto, the federal government's solution was to send them beer to help ease their pain.

From its founding until it was decommissioned in 1923, the base never engaged in military action or was given much thought. Other regiments were sent to the train and quickly left, and with each shift in military policy, fewer and fewer troops were left there. In 1914, it was primarily used as a hunting ground for the Egmont Key soldiers. The land has been a preserve,

The grounds of Fort DeSoto, where the ghosts of soldiers, children and Native Americans are seen.

a bomb testing ground, a weigh station for military surplus and a stop to get to the boat to tour another, better place. It's the fort that never knew its purpose. That is except for as a spot to bring the sick and dead.

From 1889 to 1937, the land also acted as a quarantine station for people looking to enter Tampa Bay and, if rumors are to be believed, for soldiers serving in the area who showed symptoms of disease. Originally under the umbrella of the Hillsborough County Board of Health, the number of people who ended up there grew, and buildings were constructed, moved in from other places or converted to suit the needs of a growing outbreak. Housing patients who had yellow fever was the primary focus of the hospital, and the heat and insect population did little to help those infected. In fact, it may have increased the number of fatalities and the spread of the fever.

In 1980, Fort DeSoto was home to another tragedy on a much larger scale. The Skyway Bridge runs across Tampa Bay and connects St. Petersburg and is one of the most beautiful and intimidating bridges to cross in Florida. What you see today is not the original structure, which was taken down in 1993. On the morning of May 9, 1980, freighter *MV Summit Venture* ran into a microburst, which rendered the radar useless and lowered visibility to nearly zero as it made its way into the bay. It crashed into the bridge, destroying 1,200 feet of it and sending a Greyhound bus and several other cars into the water. The accident killed thirty-five people, most of whom were housed in locations throughout Fort DeSoto during rescue and recovery and autopsy, mainly in the hospital that no longer stands on the property. The bridge has also been the site of numerous suicides and has its own hauntings attached to it.

In more modern times, the fort has had a sort of revival. There is now a state park, a historical section marking the importance of the fort to the coast and numerous charters that cast off from the location. Like most coastal towns, it is also a great place to fish if you know the right spots. There are several great locales to cast a line if you are a single lady. You might just leave with dinner for the night and a ghost for a date.

A good-looking man has been known to walk the area and approach women who are fishing by themselves. He often has a pole and gives them advice on how to catch the best fish. He might talk to them but is sometimes just seen wading out into the water or waving hello. The ladies are usually responsive to him. He's lean and muscular, with messy black hair and dark sunglasses. Then, the reports say, he will just not be there the next moment. His pole, sometimes stuck into the water or leaning up

The dock—one of the places Daulton is said to try to pick up ladies.

against something, will also be gone. Bill Miller claims that the ghost is that of Daulton Gray, a local who was well known in the community who was shot and killed in 1994. He was known as a man without a care in the world and a flirt, and descriptions of the ghost fit the descriptions of Gray. According to *The Tampa Triangle* and other online sources that might just be echoing Miller, the ghost is known to look for a date after the toll in an area known as Bunces Pass Bridge and near Potter's Peer Bait Shop, where Gray is said to have worked for a time.

Now known as Fort DeSoto Fishing Pier, Bait, and Tackle, the shop will not confirm if Gray ever worked there or if his ghost is something spoken about by locals. The new owners have never heard the legend before, and one young lady even said, "I was told to say Daulton never worked here," perhaps due to the popularity of Miller's book and stories it spawned. One interesting thing to note is that Miller describes Gray as looking casual and talking, but some recent stories online say he is looking for a specific woman, although the reports never mention her name. Perhaps a woman he loved has since died, and he is trying to find her.

Foundation of the old hospital, where the mother is said to be looking for her children.

On the other side of the spectrum is a very different kind of love. According to university professor, artist and paranormal investigator Brandy Stark, one of the saddest ghosts might be that of a grieving mother still looking for her children. When more of the base opened for quarantine duty, different buildings were used to house people with different conditions and different levels of yellow fever. Due to the quick spread of the sickness, people could be moved swiftly from one building to another, and families would be separated as the fever progressed. According to a story Stark was told, one mother was taken away from her children, and they ended up dying without her. When she heard of their deaths, her crying could be heard throughout the base. People have reported still hearing her crying and screaming as she searches the grounds for her kids. Some have even caught her voice on tape whispering about her sadness.

Things are like that at Fort DeSoto. There have been so many lives taken there that no one can quite tell who the people are. For example, in the main part of the fort, people have seen glowing lights and figures described as having a light around them who simply disappear. They are not in uniform, so they could be anyone from the history of the location. The laughing children who people talk about could be the old echoes of the Tocoboga or the Seminoles or the voices of yellow fever victims who met their end on the property. There have been figures on the beach who appear one moment and then dissolve as they walk into the water. There is even a kite flyer who can't seem to get his kite in the air and then disappears. People have also seen spirits climbing the stairs, looking confused at the cars in the parking lot and strolling the pathways on top of the base and near the armaments. Some say that they see Native Americans dressed in very little clothes, soldiers in uniform and people wearing modern clothing. Take your pick on the story that led to these spirits being trapped at the base.

One of the more widely talked about legends involves a soldier who comes out of the bay. He is soaking wet and rises out of the water and then walks into the fort. While no soldiers ever died in combat here, it is unclear if any of them ever succumbed to yellow fever or another of the diseases they complained about over the years. It does seem odd that the soldier comes out of the water, though. None of the military records tell of a soldier drowning.

The battery is where the angry ghosts are more common. The little rooms, made of shells and concrete, are little worlds unto themselves, with dark, cold corners and echoes from every step. People have felt themselves being watched and heard footsteps behind them, just to turn around and see no one there. Most of the rooms are connected to vents leading to the top of the fort, which might explain some of the noises—but not the whispers. When people stand in the rooms, they hear someone talking softly but firmly to them. Some tell of multiple people talking at once over one another and low enough to not be understood. Vents don't explain people being tapped on the shoulder—something visitors complain about often.

Fort DeSoto was a place of misery for those who served there. Every report tells of a home that people were trying to get away from, where people did not want to be in the first place. Today, it stands as a park and memorial with a cute gift shop selling cheesy souvenirs. It was not always like that, though. Look closely enough, and you'll hear the echoes of the sufferers and see the shadows of those left behind. Stay there long enough, and you just might have a frightening story to tell of a misfortune of the past. With so much darkness, it is uplifting that two of the best ghost stories from that place are really about love.

2

THE HAPPY COUPLE AT STETSON UNIVERSITY

A legend cannot exist in a vacuum. A great ghost story needs a setting to make sense. To make it connect with people, that setting needs to be something recognizable and familiar. It's no use if a legend takes place in a forest where no one has ever been, but if you transplant it to the woods behind Old Man Baker's Farm, all of a sudden, it becomes a myth the town can tell. Towers are meant to be monuments, and monuments are designed to draw the attention of all who see them. They mark great people and commemorate moments in time that leaders deem worthy to be relived and remembered. Standing like centennials, they are lightning rods for ceremonies, meetings and even romantic encounters. They are also lightning rods for ghosts and legends.

Hulley Tower may be standing at the front of the Stetson University campus in Deland, Florida, but for the students who attend it is the center of the school. Once over 116 feet tall, it has been the home to several campus legends over the years, not all of them haunted. For example, students go to the tower before a big test and rub the bricks hoping for good luck. If it is a particularly tough exam, students ask the two people interred inside the tower for help. It's also said to be the meeting place of a secret, exclusive society at the college, but no one has ever been able to get a firm handle on the real story. A first kiss between a couple in the shadow of this monument is said to secure a relationship that will last forever.

One of the creepiest legends about the tower, based on that first-kiss story but gone horribly wrong, is the story of Susanna Brown. She was said

Remains of Hulley Tower.

to be the daughter of a rich and influential Baptist minister from Iowa. She attended Stetson in the early 1890s when it was a finishing school, and in her first semester, she fell in love with her English professor. Over the course of the year, they would meet at Hulley Tower late at night to talk and spend time together. The affair continued through the summer, but things took a turn in the fall semester. While they were kissing behind the tower late one night, they were spotted by a fellow staff member. He went to the administration, and by the next afternoon, Susanna was thrown out of school, and her professor was fired.

She was destroyed. She would have to go home dishonored and without the man she loved. She cleaned out her room, making sure to take a ribbon her love had given her and a poem he had written. She snuck off to Hulley Tower and jumped from the top after telling the world that she would love her banished professor forever. To this day during the fall semester, her voice is heard declaring her passion for her lost love. Her ghost is also caught climbing the tower stairs and seen jumping from the top.

It's the kind of story you've heard before, or at least you've heard something like it wherever you're from. The legend was made popular in Dusty Smith's *Haunted Deland and the Ghosts of West Volusia County*. The trouble is, it never happened. Unlike other bits of folklore or legends, this story seems to be the creation of the author herself, although it is unclear if she was told the story by another source or was looking to explain a haunting that she had heard. It falls apart on a basic level, although all who hear it want it to be true. Brown is said to have attended the college and committed suicide in 1892 or 1893. Hulley Tower was built by the second president of the university, Lincoln Hulley, who served Stetson between 1904 and 1934, twelve years after the suicide. He and his wife, Eloise, donated the building to the university, mainly as a source for the eleven bells she loved that rang out over the campus. Both Hulleys are laid to rest in the mausoleum at the base of the tower. Lincoln Hulley died right before it was completed in 1934, and the bells continued to play there for decades after Eloise died. There is no way Brown could have killed herself by throwing herself off a tower that didn't exist.

So, maybe the suicide happened somewhere else on campus, and the tower, being a touchstone for life at Stetson, became the new site of the death. According to Kelly Larson, archivist at the college, there have been no suicides on campus. There is no story that matches Brown's on campus, and there is no death that matches Brown's or any reference to her attendance or expulsion from the school. Furthermore, the picture published in Smith's book identified a specific man as the professor who was having the affair. In fact, that man acted as an interim president for the college a few decades after the picture was taken and has a long history with the school. He was not quietly thrown out or even a professor there.

The real haunting at the tower is actually much more romantic. Lincoln and Eloise Hulley are said to still walk the grounds near the tower in the early morning hours. Although they died at different times, they found each other in death and returned to the place they loved in life. At times, they are said to be seen walking a dog, although it is more commonly said to be Lincoln Hulley walking the dog alone. It is more likely that this is another potential ghost who has been connected to Hulley because of the tower and the popularity of the love story. This legend is repeated on campus and retold by people who attended the school. There are written references to it in the school paper, and most people who went to Stetson have seen the couple or know someone

One of the remaining bells from Hulley Tower that is still said to ring.

who has. When they were considering taking the tower down several years ago, some even commented online that they hoped it would not affect the ghosts. There have also been reports of the bells sounding even though no one is ringing them—an amazing feat, considering they are not even housed in the tower anymore.

The couple might be seen other places on campus, or at least people believe their ghosts are responsible for other activity on campus. They say this is due to the bells Eloise held so close to her heart. In 2005, ninety-four feet of the tower were taken down due to safety reasons, and the bells were dispersed throughout campus, including the library and Elizabeth Hall. The bells themselves might hold some spiritual energy in them.

The bodies of the couple are still at the base of the tower. Their coffins are visible through the windows, but the building is locked, and there is no reason for staff to go inside. Before the bells were removed, the people who were responsible for ringing them would often feel a presence when they climbed the stairs. One former ringer said he would feel someone with him and sometimes a hand on his shoulder. He got into the habit of saying hello to Eloise when he went up.

Legends give birth to other legends. We need them, and we need them to be ours. We take the best parts—the ones that really speak to us—and add details to make them our own. Every generation borrows the greatest hits from the one before, until the original story, the truth of the details, is lost. Not that it matters much. A great story is often better than the truth and always better when you can be part of it. Hulley Tower inspires that kind of borrowing. Still looming large on the campus of Stetson despite its new, small stature, it continues to be the kind of place students go to feel the electricity at the school and to be part of something bigger than themselves, like a living yearbook that isn't contained to one year. It would seem some keep coming back to hear bells and relive good memories, even after they die.

3
LOVE AT THE BRIDGE

Love and hate are not opposites but rather opposite ends of a single spectrum—different sides of the same coin. They are both born and fueled by passion. To love one thing often leads to the hating of something else, and you can usually trace loathing of something back to a moment when it was loved and fell apart. When paranormal moments happen, the people experiencing it or telling the story of someone else after the fact need to choose which end of the spectrum it comes from. Sometimes the choice is easy. A man was hanged for a crime he didn't commit and comes back to haunt the people who did it to him. A woman loved her favorite piano and is heard playing it long after she is dead. The more confusing and ambiguous the haunting, the harder it is for people to decide which backstory to pick from. This is made nearly impossible when people can't even decide what the meaning of those tales might be.

It's said that no one quite knew whether Ludmilla Clark committed murder out of love or hate. Perhaps her mental health was a factor. After all, how could someone who did what she did be in their right mind? Even her husband admitted in later years that she had become so obsessed with her actions that she could no longer control herself. The way people tell her story, or at least the way the story has been handed down through the years, paints the picture of a woman who loved children. It was just a shame that she had to kill them.

The Peace River runs mostly along Route 17, but there is a stretch that is said to be anything but peaceful. It is connected, even if not physically, to

Bloody Bucket Bridge in Wauchula, Florida.

several of the legends in the area focusing on the power of springs and the potential Fountain of Youth. In Wauchula, Florida, however, the tales get a bit darker. It said that the water there runs bloodred under any full moon. The story also goes on to say that on those nights, you can hear phantom splashing and babies' cries and, on some occasions, see empty buckets on the banks fill with the tainted water.

It's all the fault of Ludmilla Clark, although she usually is not named in the story. There have also been references to her being named Mary and Martha. She was a formerly enslaved woman who came south from Georgia shortly after the Civil War and set up shop as a midwife for the growing town of Wauchula. She was good at her job and well respected for her work in the community, so what she ended up doing was even more confusing to the people of the town. Some say she became obsessed with the overpopulation of the area. After the Civil War, things were tough for everyone in the South, and even more so in Florida, which had a struggling economy and was still reeling from the Seminole Wars when the War Between the States broke out. Ludmilla believed it was in everyone's best interests to keep the population down to make the burden easier. Her love for her community led her to do bad things.

Some say love motivated her in another way. As a slave, she had seen her own children killed or sold into slavery. After moving to Wauchula and getting the only job she could, she was forced to deliver other people's children—more specifically, babies born to white families. Looking down at them and knowing she would never hold her own again slowly drove her mad, and each new child brought her closer to revenge.

Either way, the number of stillborn babies she attempted to deliver grew. In reality, Ludmilla had started killing the children, and the more she got away with it, the more careless she became, until the people of the town grew suspicious. The death of a newborn was not unusual in those days, and sentimentality for the dead was dulled. Rather than burying the dead children at family or town cemeteries, they allowed her to bury the bodies by the river while she was disposing of the afterbirth. That was why the river started to become red at times, although back then, only Ludmilla would see it.

Although nothing could ever be proven, whispers spread throughout the town. People stopped going to her to deliver their children, causing her to become even more detached from reality. According to her husband, she still made her trips to the same spot, but this time, she dumped empty buckets into the water. Try as she could to get it all out, the pails would fill again with bloody water, and the crying voices of the children she had killed drowned out the voice of her husband telling her there was nothing in the water or in the buckets. She became obsessed, traveling to the bridge more and more often and trying to comfort the cries. It became too much, and she eventually committed suicide in the water, although other stories say she lost her balance, fell in and died.

View from where the bodies are said to have been dumped.

A few years later, people walking across the bridge began to hear a wailing coming from the banks of the Peace River. They heard the cries of children and would rush to the water to see what was wrong, only to hear the cries from somewhere else nearby. Even more unexplained, the water in that part of the river would appear red during the full moon, and if you placed an empty bucket near the river's edge, it would fill up with red water. It was around then that people in the town renamed the stretch of road they knew as Rhinehart Road to Bloody Bucket Road and the crude bridge that ran into Main Street to Bloody Bucket Bridge.

Red flags raise as you hear this story, but it has become one of the most published bits of folklore coming out of that area of Florida. Why was she not killed or at least thrown in jail for her crimes? As she was a Black woman living in the South, it would not have been out of the ordinary. Why did it take so long to figure out the story? Why did the people turn her crimes into a tribute?

Perhaps the most popular account of the story comes from 2005's *Weird Florida* by Charlie Carlson. It appears to be the first published version of the legend. He records several witnesses to some of the cries from the woods near Bloody Bucket Bridge on nights of the full moon. Since then, the story has been retold in newspaper articles, websites and other books, with the details changed slightly but always telling of a woman and her twisted love.

The street is now officially known as Griffin Road, the bridge Griffin Road Bridge and the area that was once her dumping ground is a boat launch into the Peace River. The surrounding bank drops off quickly, with only large stones in the water to balance yourself to get under the bridge. The spot is anything but quiet, with continual traffic, slow but steady, and local animal life, especially alligators and birds.

A common ghostly motif is crying at a haunted bridge, much like the story of the Bellamy Bridge in Marianna, Florida. This is a much more romantic version of a ghost story and more well known in the state. There was once a woman named Elizabeth who lost her life near there. She had just married one of the prominent members of Jackson County, Dr. Samuel C. Bellamy. One version of the story speaks of her beginning to dance too wildly at her wedding reception. Another version says she retired to her bedroom to take a nap. In both, her dress catches fire, and she is soon consumed in flames and screaming. Although people rushed to her aid, it was too late, and the burns were too severe. She died a few days later and was buried in the family plot owned by her brother-in-law, Dr. Edward Bellamy, on the banks of the Chipola River.

Bellamy Bridge. *Photo courtesy of Mark and Kari Muncy of Eerie Florida.*

Samuel was devastated by the death of his new bride and would visit her grave often. Eventually, he stopped going, although the pain never truly ended. Perhaps missing him or wanting to comfort him, Elizabeth began to rise from the grave some nights and walk along the banks looking for him. She could be seen on Edward's property and along the water, and when the bridge was eventually built, she was also seen on the bridge getting in the way of cars. Later, other elements of the paranormal were added to the story. Along with the visions came crying heard from near the water. The source of the sound could never be identified.

The story has become one of the most popular ghost stories in Florida, with legend trippers and paranormal investigators making their way to that part of the state every year to try to see the woman. The tale, however, is actually a work of fiction based on real people. The couple really did exist and lived in the area. Elizabeth did not die on her wedding night but years after of disease, probably yellow fever, only a week before her son Alexander passed away from the same sickness. That might be enough grief to cause a ghost, and from multiple reports over the years, you would have to believe the vision and the crying are true. The exaggerated backstory, however, is the work of fiction writer Caroline Lee Hentz, who lived in the area. In her book *Ernest Linwood*, otherwise known as *The Long Moss*, there is a story that echoes the folklore events of the Bellamys, although it appears that she got the story from events that happened in Georgia. Hentz claimed that it really happened, and because she often wrote about her adopted home of Marianna and because the name she used in the story was Bellamy, people eventually embraced the fictional account.

There are many natural reasons why something that looks like a person might be seen on a bridge or near a swamp, but the connecting aspect of Bellamy Bridge and Bloody Bucket Bridge is the sound of someone crying. This repeats itself around the country and around the world. In the paranormal community, it is known as the Crybaby Bridge phenomenon. Scientists believe the sound is not anything spooky or otherworldly but rather the sound of running water over rock, foundations and vegetation. People associate it with the human sounds because we are wired to process information against something we know, and every overly alert parent knows that any noise you hear sounds like a kid crying.

Most of the firsthand accounts from Bloody Bucket Bridge involve the noises. The rumors of red water, which can't be traced to a source, could be runoff of minerals during certain times of the month. The question remains about why the area, of all the potential spots along the Peace River, gained fame and a nickname. The police officer who stopped me when we went to check on the legend offered an explanation for the name Bloody Bucket Road. It was one that I had already heard connected to the story and several others like it. The officer said, "It was a tough bar. Every night there were fights....People being hauled off. People hated to work there because every night when it closed, they had to clean the floors, and the wash bucket was filled with all the blood."

It was the rough-and-tumble bar named the Big Apple at the end of the street—now just a slab of concrete overgrown with grass and covered with

All that remains of the famous Bloody Bucket bar.

trucking equipment—that gave the street its sinister nickname. The bar was eventually closed, and the road went back to being Griffin Road, although a few locals still passed around the old name as a reminder of the good old days before the town was dry. By the turn of the twenty-first century, enough people still remembered the nickname to give the stories a ring of truth.

Of course, this doesn't account for the midwife or the dead children written about by Carlson and other modern writers. On Halloween 2003, two years before *Weird Florida* was first published, a blogger known as Cindi circulated a ghost story on the website Country Living, Country Skills, titled "The Legend of Bloody Bucket Road." She explains how an old, disabled Black man sitting outside the 7-Eleven nearby told her the story. She was brought to task in the comments of the story about how many of the physical details of the story are off, until she eventually came back and said the story was fiction. She had always heard the name Bloody Bucket Road and wanted to write her own version of how it got its name.

The majority of people who gave feedback to her seemed to be fans of her work and understood the legend was made up without being told, but there were enough people who responded to allow that story to take on a life of its own. It's unclear whether Carlson, the man who really solidifies the story in *Weird Florida*, was working off Cindi's blog or if he was a victim of hearing someone repeat the story that they had heard from someone else. Unfortunately, he is no longer with us, but everyone I spoke to, including his son, says he was an honest reporter of the unknown and a respected researcher.

Elizabeth and Ludmilla, or Mary or Martha if you prefer, are kindred spirits in a way. Part of their stories are oceans apart—one a rich woman who married a doctor and the other a former enslaved woman driven to mental illness. In death though, they find a common ground in their sadness and their loneliness. Both loved and lost, and those emotions are strong enough to make their spirits restless. Both continue to linger in our minds when the noises start and reflections make our eyes see things that aren't there. Whether from a place of romance, community well-being or the love of a child, passion is the fire that flips the coin. Maybe that's why we see both sides of it when something unexplained happens on that bridge down the street.

4
LOVE AND LEGACY AT OAK RIDGE

Nothing is stronger than the bonds of family. Through celebration and calamity, they are the ones who are supposed to be with you no matter what. You lean on them, and they learn to rely on you because that's what families do. That may not end when someone dies. In fact, that deep bond might be the kind of emotion that makes someone stick around to make sure everything is okay. Family business is never over. There are three families, their stories as different as their memorials in the cemetery, who have been linked to haunted legends at Oak Ridge Cemetery in Arcadia, Florida. And all three stories are different forms of that love and a link to the haunted history of the city.

The first might be the most well-known legend of the county, mainly because of its link to one of the worst crimes in the area's history. In 1967, all seven of the Richardson children died mysterious deaths over the course of two days. The final autopsy determined that the kids had been poisoned by pesticide. Their father, James Richardson, was convicted of the crime and served decades in jail before being exonerated. The details of the case, such as him placing down payments on their Christmas bikes, brushing their hair and sneaking them their favorite candies, tell of a man who truly loved his children and not someone who would have killed them for $1,000 each. It was a case of being railroaded and being too poor to afford the best defense, especially as a Black man living in the South. The next-door neighbor and babysitter, Bessie Reese, initially confessed to intentionally feeding them the tainted lunch at the time of the investigation, and then on her death bed told her family again how and why she had done it. Although she had confessed to the crime, she was considered unstable and was not even brought in as a witness, though she had been with them during the time of the poisoning.

The children, who ranged from ages two to eight, are buried at the cemetery and are thought to be the source of several stories of hauntings. Goat Hill, several miles to the north of the cemetery, is known for its ghost lights. Sometimes at night, people see an odd light, compared to an early sunset, coming from the direction of the cemetery over the hill. There have been reports of orbs of light seen by the human eye and caught on camera, which is not

The talking statue in Oak Ridge Cemetery.

all that uncommon in ghost reports. However, people have reported seeing half a dozen that appear to be playing with one another. The children do not contain their games to Goat Hill, though. Over the years, children in the neighborhood have spoken of playing with kids in the cemetery who eventually disappear as they hide behind headstones. One story even says you can make them come out during the day by covering your eyes near their graves and counting to thirty.

By all reports, the children have no adult supervision and are allowed to roam free. That kind of motherly care is reserved for the Talking Mary statue located in another part of the cemetery. In a plot of land reserved for the Hollingsworth family, there is a stone statue that has been known to talk to the children of the neighborhood. The Hollingsworths are an important family in the modern history of Arcadia. They made their money in fruit and agriculture, and there are memorials and markers throughout the town emphasizing their prominence. The family, it seems, is important enough to be looked in on after death, as well. The plot, which currently has eight markers in addition to the statue, is the final resting spot of the first- and second-generation members who impacted the community.

The statue itself is actually St. Agnes holding orchids. St. Agnes is one of the most popular of the Christian saints and is the patron of girls and purity. This fits with the legend, as the voices are most often heard by young females who are somehow drawn to the statue. The woman, set at an odd angle to

Mary, or Agnes, looking over the Hollingsworth family.

look over the people in the plot, is worn and missing fingers but is still said to be taking care of the family and the ideals of their upbringing. People notice that the statue is always colder than the stones in any other part of the area and talk of the smell of incense being burned, which immediately goes away when they start to walk away from her.

Children are said to have entire conversations with her, but most of the other accounts are sporadic occurrences, happening randomly and with no specific connection to people or times. They never reveal what she says to them, even years later, but the folklore encourages young ladies to go to her for advice or counsel. She is also said to instruct them to look after her family's gravesite.

The most likely suspect for the guardian of her family is Bertie Louise Hollingsworth, who died in 1924. She is the oldest of the females there, and the story has been part of the community for years. The only Mary Hollingsworth is Mary Naomi, but by the time of her death in 1970, people had already started spreading the word on the mysterious whispers. Paranormal investigators and legend trippers frequent the site and often get voices on tape, known as Electronic Voice Phenomena (EVP), while talking to her. There is a deep tradition of talking statues in cemeteries, most of them Mary and Agnes, so it's not unusual that this one, especially at such an odd position, would become the subject of a haunting and a legend. Skeptics say that the voices are nothing more than the wasps that like to make a home in her armpit, but those who had conversations with her when they were children cannot be convinced that she is not some matriarch of the family still doing her duty for her clan.

While not a traditional family, the military is known to form the same kinds of bonds, with those who served calling their fellow soldiers, sailors and pilots brothers and sisters. The bond is even stronger when those soldiers are in a foreign land or lost brothers and sisters together. The real centerpiece of Oak Ridge is a memorial to the British Royal Air Force (RAF) pilots who trained and died in Florida during the World War II era. This is a part of Florida history that is not known by many. After the famous speech in which Winston Churchill proclaimed, "Give us the tool and we will finish the job," Franklin Roosevelt passed the Lend-Lease Act, which led to the Arnold Plan. British pilots were allowed to train in the United States because the skies over their own country were too dicey to allow new pilots to get the experience they needed. Arcadia petitioned to use Carlstrom Field.

The first class of RAF pilots graduated in 1941 but were not without their issues. Many of the foreigners were not used to the hazing that was part of American troop training, and it damaged their morale. As explained in *RAF Wings over Florida* by Will Largent, many of the trainees also suffered from homesickness and overindulgence. It seems that the young men had come from a land of war and sacrifice into a land of plenty, and many were

overwhelmed with how much food and how many Florida oranges they were able to get at a moment's notice. It would also seem that they were distracted by the number of Florida women with "loose morals" who they could also find at a moment's notice. Even given the distractions, many of the airmen went on to distinguish themselves in combat. Twenty-three of them,

Opposite: Graves of the brave RAF pilots who lost their lives in Arcadia.

Left: Infamous disappearing Union Jack.

however, died in training in or near Arcadia and are buried at Oak Ridge Cemetery, along with their instructor, John Paul Riddle, who requested to be buried with his men forty years after he helped train them. The cemetery is their final resting spot and hosts a memorial commemorating Arcadia and the fallen pilots' contribution to history.

The stories of the memorial are traditional haunted folklore for soldiers' graves. People are seen standing before the headstones and then disappear moments later. A dark figure is said to move from grave to grave, mourning each and leaving memorials, much like the legend of the man who leaves flowers at Edgar Allan Poe's grave in Baltimore. When approached, he disappears, and the things he left are no longer by the graves. There are also reports of phantom planes, sometimes seen but mostly heard, above the cemetery—maybe explained away by airports nearby, many of which host airshows that feature World War II planes.

It makes sense that these stories might not be merely legend. Part of the mythology of the paranormal includes spirits being at rest. These pilots would be more likely to walk their graves because they are not buried in their own country but in a foreign one, far from home. They might not be able to find peace or find their way back to their own families, especially given the lore of spirits not being able to cross water in motion.

One of the other unusual stories involves the Union Jack flying at the memorial. People have reported that the flag sometimes disappears, although no one is there to remove it. According to reports, the flag was raised and lowered daily, but after the original caretaker of the memorial died, the cemetery stopped taking it down. It is supposed to fly at all times. Legend says that the Union Jack disappears or is moved to half-mast while people are visiting, even though there is no visible caretaker present. People can take pictures of it, and when they look at them after, the flag is gone or changed.

People go to cemeteries to be close to those who have passed. Standing there among the stone and grass, they tell their beloved dead that they are still thinking about them and looking after their memory and legacy. There are places, like Oak Ridge Cemetery, that allow us to understand it happens the other way too. In death, love and duty do not fade. The dead may continue to look after one another, enjoy quiet moments reliving their shared history or get one more game in before being called home. That's what family does.

5

THE SINGING MANATEE RIVER

S tart from a basic premise, an understanding we can all agree to before the details of the stories are told. There is a stretch of the Manatee River that runs through Bradenton, Florida, that has been experiencing something unexplained for hundreds of years through different cultures and different times. Step into the story of the Singing River knowing people have been able to explain parts of it. Scientists can take a look at what happens there and tell you there is nothing going on they can't explain, but they'll also avoid the parts that confuse them or don't make sense. Even if the legend gets murky at times or keeps changing, it does not mean the mysterious figures seen on the water are not really there or that the voices people have heard for hundreds of years are nothing but nature. Go into this story understanding one thing: the river is haunted.

The next thing to decide is which part if the haunting to focus on. You can spend time consumed by trying to figure out why mysterious music seems to rise from the water itself. Maybe you can focus on the ghostly figures seen in the water and on the banks and decide whether you think they are the result of a massive suicide or the souls of people called back to the spot after death to drink of the mysteriously addictive water. Be careful not to overlook the phantom canoe seen in the spring that is said to be sailing to meet with a lover on the other side. When you've gotten all that straight in your head, you must deal with the phantom pirate ship a woman destroyed to escape a song she didn't want to hear.

Singing River in Bradenton, Florida.

At some point, you'll come to realize they are all just different versions of the same stories, and all of them are love stories.

It might be best to begin with one that sounds the most familiar. The young daughter of a Calusa chief meets the son of a Timucuan leader, and the two quickly fall in love. The only place the two could ever see each other was at the Manatee River in Bradenton, which was considered neutral territory for both tribes. He lived north of the river, and she lived south, so they met in the middle at night and fed the love they knew their families would not bless. When he asked for her hand in marriage, she told him of the mystic spring on her side of the water. Anyone who has ever taken a drink—and she has often—will never be able to survive without the water of their homeland. They will forever yearn for it and will never be quenched until they have it again. Still, she reluctantly agreed to marry him, and at that moment, the water came alive. The low hum turned into a song, until the two were completely surrounded by music coming from the river itself. The young man got ready to jump over the side of their canoe because he was so scared, but she gently held his arm. She told him this was the music of her ancestors, heard only during certain times of the year and when their voices were needed. The singing was blessing their love.

The two decided to move to his side of the river, as his family was more accepting. Here is where the legend takes one of several different paths. In the most popular version, they lived happily together as Timucua, but she still felt the pull to her people. Eventually, she returned, and her father accepted their love and vowed the young man would take over as chief of the tribe when he died. Already being the chief on his side of the river, it united them, which explains why the Timucua basically disappeared from history before the coming of the Seminoles. The other variation also has a happy ending—but not before bloodshed. On the Calusa side, her leaving was seen as a kidnapping, and a war ensued. Many were killed before a truce was struck, and they all drank of the spring and were overcome by the music.

This story is used to explain why centuries of people heard an odd hum coming from the river, which they described as singing. The different tribes heard it. The European settlers heard it. In fact, according to published accounts in diaries and newspaper articles, the mysterious noise was heard until recent times—as late as the early 1900s. Every culture had its swing at the story, which was also connected to the ghostly figures seen in the water. The music isn't heard anymore, but to this day, people tell of canoes on the water that disappear and specters walking on the surface of the river. There are people seen on the shores who vanish without responding to people calling out to them and different-sized orbs that bounce off the water on clear nights. Then there is the large shadow seen under the water that people say looks like a large boat trying to rise out of the water.

Another question about the couple's tale is whether it's too familiar to have any truth to it or if it's even a Native American story at all. The young

The best view from the Calusa side to where the lights and the pirate ship are seen.

lovers who are kept apart, the warring families, the secret meeting and the eventual reconciliation—it's a familiar story. But there is also something about the singing that keeps bouncing around in your head like a song that you can't quite remember the melody to.

Two books explored the story in the 1980s and seemed to reawaken the old tale as a reason for the experiences people were having. The first was *Ghosts Won't Cross Water and the Walls Speak* by Nan Russell in 1983 and the other was *The Singing River* by Joe Warner in 1986. Both of these make reference to the even older printed versions of the legend, including 1933's *The Lure of the Manatee* by Lillie Brown McDuffee and a mysterious article published in the *Bradenton Times* in 1945. All of these point to a story told for a long time that borrows from other stories as time goes on.

A reporter for the *Bradenton Herald* named Jack Leffingwell took the legend to task in 1945, concluding that the music was "tannic acid washing off the palmetto roots in the rainy season into the river, setting up a chemical reaction with the fuller's earth on the riverbed."

Julia Martin, a chemist living in the Boston area, summarized it, stating, "When the acid/base reaction happens, it produces gas as a byproduct like carbon dioxide and oxygen. The gas rapidly evolving produces a sound we can hear audibly. Like an Alka Seltzer tablet in water or some acidic beverage. You will hear it fizz as the gas turbulently escapes the liquid solution." Sounds like a pretty decent explanation for the natural oddity heard by the Calusa, the Timucua and the Seminoles, who reported hearing the odd music and thought it was the spirits of those who had passed.

A possible explanation, if you don't like science, was given by Laura Hildick Burge, author of a series of books called *The Singing River Story*. She had chosen to center her romance novels on a Pascagoula legend from Mississippi known to her family and spread widely in that part of the country. Burge also has family living in Holiday, Florida, a little more than an hour away from Bradenton, and her story reflects what the Calusa princess tells her suitor.

The legend explains where the music comes from, although sometimes the answer is more confusing than the question. The Biloxi and Pascagoula had a tentative peace between them until the chief of the Pascagoula fell in love with a woman promised to the chief of the Biloxi. This was so offensive that war was declared. The Pascagoula, knowing the Biloxi made slaves of the people they conquered and knowing there was no way they could win a war between the tribes, killed themselves by walking into the water and drowning. As they marched to the water, they all sang a sad song, which is the music heard coming from the water to this day.

The legend is told by several different tribes in different locations and is enough of a tradition that there have been multiple studies made of it. That said, some parts still seem odd. Why did the chief not just give himself up or deny his love based on what was good for his tribe? The mass suicide of the tribe seems like a possible explanation for why they disappeared rather than a rational response to drama with their neighbors.

There are other issues with the legend specific to the Manatee River. One of the prime locations to hear the singing was known as Rocky Bluff and is mentioned in several different versions of the story. The problem is that Rocky Bluff is on the northern side of the river. Why would you be able to hear the singing on the Timucuan side of the water, and if you could, why did the young lover not know about it? Also, the story does not conform with actual Timucua politics that say leadership is determined from the mother's side of the family and not the father's. The young lover would not have been made chief but rather his cousin would have. This all points to the story being European, or at least a story retold by the strangers from across the sea who changed it to fit their understanding of the people they were meeting. This means they were also hearing the singing and seeing the ghosts in the water and wanted to understand where it was coming from.

They went one step further and made up their own version based on the things they feared. This story is said to be passed down by the Egmont Key Lighthouse keeper and constant contributor to local folklore, Captain Charles Moore. Pascual Miquel, also known as the Butcher, took the daughter of a Spanish captain stationed in Pensacola and shipped her off to his secret hiding place at the Manatee River. The young lady, named Carlotta or Charlotta, was not a willing girlfriend, but the Butcher was so in love that he would do anything to please her. Knowing she was a great lover of music, he strung harp strings from the windows of the cabin where she was being held prisoner. Every time the winds blew, he promised her, "You will hear beautiful music." The first time he took off to bury his loot near Rocky Bluff, she escaped from the cabin and found herself in the middle of a river she could not swim across. Knowing she might never be rescued, she made her way to the hull of the ship where the munitions were kept. She set them on fire and sunk it. Her screams were drowned out by the sound of the wind going through the harp strings as Miquel watched from the bluff. Moore explains that this is why the music is heard and why the dark figure of a ship is still seen on the water.

Carlotta, in another version of the story, escapes and sneaks down to the hull of the ship. She begins to pierce holes in it, until it starts to sink. Again, her screams are heard as she drowns. Miquel, who had been off preparing for Carlotta's dad to rescue her, sails back into the river just in time to see the ship disappear below the surface. He buried what treasure he had at Rocky Bluff and left, planning to come back. Legend has it that he was never able to return to the spot, and every time he tried, the music would get so loud that it would rock his boat and make the men fall over in pain. Someone else, maybe a descendant of one of the crew, came back years later under the cover of night and used dynamite to break open the bluff and take the treasure, which was reported to have happened less than one hundred years ago.

Many of the ghosts on the water are also attributed to the disappearance of the spring, which drew so many back to the village they loved. The Calusa princess had warned her boyfriend of it, and the town grew up around it, but there seems to be little trace of the water supply today. In fact, the spring

The view of the Singing River from the haunted Braden Castle ruins.

does still exist, although it bears nothing to suggest its former importance. It's hidden away in the Manatee Historic Park under a shed. Most of it was paved over to make room for the double road that crosses between it and the Manatee River. Hidden away between K.W. "King" Wiggins General Store and Manatee County's first courthouse, pretty much forgotten about, you'll find the only remaining fragment of the Calusa's greatest treasure. Its drying up might also be why there are so many other ghosts spoken about in the immediate area, including a semitransparent man who walks the road looking confused and lost.

There has always been something mysterious about the water. For something that is so common but such a vital part of our life, there are aspects of it that still confuse us and demand to be understood. We know so little and get our information from observation, like the way the moon hits it at night or how the tides seem to move like our emotions. Much like love, it is the ultimate metaphor for the misunderstood pieces of ourselves, which is why ghost stories and legends about both seem to ebb and flow like the passions of people themselves. And just as people will keep falling in love, they'll keep telling stories about the water trying to make sense of it all.

6

LOVING YOUR SCHOOL;
LOVING YOUR JOB

It doesn't take long on the campus of the University of Florida before you learn "Alma Mater" and "Orange and Black." Most people there have probably been singing it for years before they ever entered college. The same can be said for "High O'er Towering Pines" and "Hymn to the Garnet and Gold" at Florida State University in Tallahassee. These songs are part of the fabric of the schools, the institutions that bond the students and alumni together and make them part of something bigger, reaching back through the years and moving them forward. That's how traditions are born, and taking part in these rituals connects people. Every freshman must walk the library stairs three times before their first class, and every time a virgin graduates, a stone falls from a tower. These rituals offer initiation and write and rewrite the history of the colleges as each new class goes through them. Haunted folklore does the same, so there's no surprise that between the touching of a statue's toes and dunking a boy who has lost his virginity in the fountain, colleges embrace their haunted history.

Stop a student walking to English composition, and chances are they can tell you some story of ghosts in one of the dorms or the library or walking one of the fields after a game. These stories are as much a part of student life as frat parties and homecoming. It makes sense too. Many colleges are the anchors of towns and remain constant for decades. A dorm may be remodeled, but the building has been there for generations. That allows generations of people to have suffered tragedy and even death and for simple stories to change and evolve. Between stress and new love and the excitement

College campuses are known for their haunted love stories.

students feel as they get to learn their school, there exist all the earmarks for psychic energy to be trapped in the stone buildings—if you believe in that kind of thing. Colleges need their ghosts, but sometimes when you hear the right story, the ghosts need their college. That connection and that duty, even more than a traumatic event, can inspire loyalty even after death.

A perfect example is the story of Steve on the University of Florida campus. There are many ghosts alleged to haunt Gainesville, but Steve is one spirit who is said to return to his job every day because of his love of the students. One of the oldest buildings on campus, Thomas Hall, is also one of the most beautiful and offers a link to the past that some of the newer ones don't. This may be what adds to the setting of the ghost story. Years ago, students didn't have to leave the building to get a good meal because their dining hall was on the bottom floor. Steve, who ran the kitchen, was a loud man who could be heard during meals banging pots and pans and yelling at the staff. The students who lived here heard him before going on to their classes, and he became something of a fixture and folk hero to the dorm. The story says that Steve died a sudden death, some say in the kitchen, and it hit the students hard.

They did not have to wait long to connect with him again. Shortly after his passing, students and staff would hear yelling and banging in the kitchen that they could not explain. Some stories say they even recognized old Steve's voice. Authorities at the University of Florida say Thomas Hall's kitchen was run by a man named Steve and that the stories are more of a tribute to the man than a genuine ghost. The people who spread the story say they know for sure who it is. The odd noises continued even after the dorm changed and the kitchen and dining hall was moved out of the building. The whole thing might be more of a case of bad heating radiators and air conditioning vents, but then there are those pesky voices they hear.

Sarah Cawthon felt the same compulsion after death to return to her job, even though she never actually worked in the building that now bears her name. All of the old stories say that Cawthon was dedicated to her job and loved the girls under her care. In 1919, after taking the job of dean of the College Home for the then Florida State College of Women, she instilled in the women under her care a love of rituals and traditions—something the school lost after her retirement in 1925. The last years of her job were the hardest for her. She was said to have been too formal at times and did not like the changes in the girls that the Roaring Twenties brought to the campus. Unable to handle their new freedoms and lifestyles, she went insane and had to be sent to a nearby asylum, although that has pretty much been discredited. Either way, she had a reputation for being difficult with the girls in her final years. She died in 1942, but her passion stayed with the campus, and every woman who had her position after was in her shadow.

Her spirit might have stayed on campus as well. Her ghost was seen almost immediately after the dedication of the resident hall that now bears her name in 1948. People would say they saw her walking in the halls as a shiny figure they always described as looking after them. Others have said they found cigarettes or liquor bottles missing and attributed them to her because of her distaste for them. Occurrences picked up a year later when the college was made coed. While men were not allowed in the dorms, some still snuck in or hung out by the building. They were met with pushes and more missing objects.

Over the years, the dorm integrated, and the activity increased. One of the other urban legend ghosts on the campus is said to be that of a girl who died while sunbathing on the roof. She was caught in a storm, and she could not get the door open and pounded on it to be let in. She was hit with lightning and died. Her ghost is said to still bang on the door, appear in windows and mirrors and be heard screaming, especially when a lightning storm hits. Many people attribute the increase in ghost sightings and odd occurrences to this young lady and not Cawthon, but it's hard to tell which ghost is which. There was a lightning strike that hit the dorm in July 1952. It caused damage to the roof and chimney, but no one was hurt, making the story of the young lady more of a cautionary tale than a genuine story of a ghost. One of the most common reports is messing with the water. Showers turn on and off by themselves, and faucets play games with the students. Maybe the two ghosts are in it together.

Elizabeth Stetson might be the most popular ghost on the campus of Stetson University in DeLand, Florida, and the building that bears her name is said to be the most haunted. The students still talk freely about her presence on campus today, especially since she was only whispered about for decades, perhaps due to the school's close affiliation with the Baptist Church, which essentially founded the college in the late 1800s. Resident assistants were even instructed to not talk about her presence back in the day, but they now make it part of their introduction to the school. When they talk about hauntings, the conversation is usually dominated by the odd things that happen at Elizabeth Hall. While the frequency of the sightings and experiences hints that there might actually be a ghost there, who it might be is the subject of legend.

Most agree that the spirit is Elizabeth Stetson, or Ms. Elizabeth as they call her, the wife of one of the founders of the school. Authorities will tell you that she actually spent little time in the building itself when she was alive. The first structure built on campus in 1892, it remains the center of campus life, filled with classrooms, meeting rooms and professor offices. Maybe this diversity makes it the best way for her to check up on all the goings-on of the campus. Perhaps it was the same love John B. Stetson had for his wife when he named the building after her that forces her to come back and look in on things.

Elizabeth Hall at Stetson University.

Either way, students and staff report odd smells at times and temperature changes that don't make sense. The building is old, so that might contribute to their stories, but that does not explain the footsteps on the stairs or the sensation of being watched. People hear clear voices on the third floor with no one there and footsteps coming from the attic when it is empty and attribute all of this to Ms. Elizabeth. Doors open and close with unseen hands, and lights often seem to have a mind of their own. One student claimed to be in the building after dark and had to travel to the third floor to get something. As she walked up the dimly lit stairs, the lights turned on around her as she made progress. The same thing happened as she traveled down the hallway. It was only after the fact that she was told they were not on a motion sensor.

Stetson, unlike other ghosts, has actually appeared to many people over the years. She is described as looking pretty and wearing a light-colored dress, although some people just get a glimpse of her out of the corners of their eyes or see her as a passing shadow. They call out to her, and she vanishes. Sometimes, though, she stays around long enough to interact with them. A few years ago, a janitor was working on the landing between the second and third floors. He had gotten in early to work—about three or four o'clock in the morning. As with most of the custodian staff and groundskeepers, he had heard all of the stories of the haunted location on campus and even felt like he was being watched when working at Elizabeth Hall. As he looked up, he saw an older, attractive woman looking down at him, smiling. He described the dress as not what the kids were wearing at the time, and he immediately knew it was Ms. Elizabeth. She then turned and disappeared as he watched. From then on, he always said hello to her when he entered the building.

One of the librarians had her own experience in the building. The halls are protected by large storm doors that close slowly when there is an emergency or a power outage—something that happens often in Florida summer storms. One day when the librarian was in Elizabeth Hall, the power went out, and she was left in the hallway watching the storm doors close. As they were almost shut, she and a student saw a figure run across the hall. She recalls, "I saw something at the end of the hall. It scooted by as the door closed. We checked a few minutes later and nobody was there." She insists that at that time of day and that time of the year, no one could have left without her seeing it.

It's worth noting that all three of these ghosts haunt buildings that have the deepest history in their colleges. All three were strong figures—fixtures in the

The third-floor landing, where Ms. Elizabeth is often seen.

school and founders in the early years of the colleges. Their stories echo the histories of the schools themselves—their buildings are shrines to tradition, and their legends are part of getting to know the school. Many places hate when people talk about their ghosts, and authorities roll their eyes when outsiders ask about them. On college campuses, there is a realization that holding on to the past sometimes means embracing the legends that act as foundations to campus life as much as the stone from the buildings. Believing in ghost stories, especially about the people who loved their campus so much, is as easy as learning the school song.

7

THE MANY LOVE STORIES
OF SILVER SPRINGS

A magician stands before you with a beautiful diamond in his hand. He closes his fist tight, waves his magic wand and, with a flash of a smile, opens his hand to reveal that the diamond is gone. You clap and hold your breath. He waves the wand again, and the diamond reappears. The trick is complete, and if you were to watch the performer closely enough, you might have noticed the sleight of hand. If you have seen the trick enough times, you might have figured out details to know how he did it. The diamond never really went anywhere, but there is that part of you that wants the trick to be real despite the logical part of your brain telling you it just isn't true.

They say the first thing that drew people to Silver Springs was the clarity of the water. It offered a look at a world most people never experience and the chance to see what was hidden in the lakes and ponds and muddy rivers they were used to. Everything was out in the open. But there was another draw to the springs. This one was darker and exotic but just as magnetic. It was said that you could reach out and touch an unknowable, untamed world before going back to the water and finding peace—the perfect balance between light and dark. That's what was sold on the shores and promoted in the fliers, and although the stories shifted and the advertisements changed their fonts, you were always being sold those two sides of the coin. You believed the trick because you wanted it to be true.

The haunted history of Silver Springs State Park exists for the same reason. It's a ghost story but also fertile grounds for the telling and revising of legends that try to explain some of those spooky tales. The two get so

Silver Springs.

mixed up and married to each other that it's hard to figure out where one legend begins and the next one starts, like an old soap opera that keeps switching out characters and the actors who play them but still relies on the drama to keep you viewing.

There are two kinds of ghost stories that come out of the amusement park in Silver Springs, Florida. One shows up in different forms in books and websites, morphing and borrowing bits of narrative from other tales and redefining itself with each generation. It's somewhat forgotten by those who work there, but each version is sworn to be true by the person who shares it. It's nonspecific and familiar and has roots in actual locations you can see and feel. It stretches through centuries, and trying to unlock what might be true and what might be legend can get you caught in rabbit holes and internet threads.

The beautiful water of the springs is said to inspire love and an entire collection of ghost legends.

Then there is the other kind of ghost story. This one is more subtle and shared only between the people who work there. They'll tell you if you ask, and everyone seems to have one, but people have stopped asking. They are modern and oddly accepted by the people who have lived through them. They are anything but legend. When trying to make sense of them, they always come back to a love story.

Silver Springs, like the legends that are born there, has one foot in history and one in the present and trips trying to decide where the surest footing is. Even its history has been revised and retold enough times to confuse the facts. The stories say the spring was home to different tribes, and over the years, different Native Americans have laid claim to it. Many still talk of it being more of a meeting place for different tribes, called the Peace Camp, and in the early days, no single people laid claim to it.

As far as documentation goes, the years after the Civil War seem to begin the modern era of Silver Springs. Before then, there are various stories told about the conflicts between the Native Americans in the area and the Europeans coming across the state. According to Tom Hollis's book *Glass Bottom Boats and Mermaid Tails*, the modern history of the area began when the steamboats came down the Ocklawaha River and basked in the beauty of the water and "barbaric" nature of the shore. Soon a hotel was built. Around this time, people were drawn to the romantic nature of the location.

There was something about a hotel in the jungle and the moonlit water at night that made it a destination for young lovers coming from different parts of the state. It was during this time that the legends of the area began to make their way into the minds of the guests, and with so many natural but unexplained marvels around them, people needed these stories to understand their environment.

Love, however, can only bring in so much money. In the 1920s, William Carl Ray and W.C. Davidson bought the land. It started with the glass-bottom boats that allowed people an even closer look at the clear waters and the beauty they held. Then the attractions came in one by one to give people more to do when they got to Silver Springs and more chances for the concessions to make money. Ray and Davidson built it into a full-blown amusement park, and before Disney World, it held the title of the most popular attraction in Florida.

If you ask some, the real hauntings in the park began with the arrival of herpetologist Ross Allen in 1930. He set up camp and brought the exotic wildlife of Florida up close to the visitors. Originally, he offered just the animals, but by 1935, he had set up the Seminole Indian Village as part of his show. Some old-timers say the village offended people of the tribe and created restless spirits, while others say the expansion brought by attractions like Ross's disturbed something in the land itself.

At this point, the Indian burial ground idea has been used and reused so many times that it might have lost impact, but Wanda, a longtime employee of the park who has seen decades of change, says there's more to it. She maintains that they need supervision to do anything on the property because there is so much Native American heritage buried under the park. Though, "I'm not saying mounds or graves, just history of the people who were here." She claims the stories of the Peace Camp are true and that Silver Springs holds a special and scared place for different tribes throughout the South. Something about the way the owners were treating the land changed that. "Back then, some used to say the Seminole Village was not a very nice thing. It may have offended some spirits who were here."

"They used to have a Seminole Village that was popular," says Bob, a ranger in the park. "Now it's just rotting away." Some people think this neglect is an affront. The Seminole culture was used and then tossed aside like the waterpark on the property that has been forced to close because it is too expensive to maintain. While this may seem like the kind of finger-pointing that just allows different sides to support their beliefs and agendas, there is something deeper at work. Step back from the *why* for a moment and realize that they would not need to find a *why* if something wasn't going on.

After the 1930s and the expansion of the park, business boomed. Silver Springs had a dream to sell and knew how to do it. It appeared in several documentaries and made a cottage industry out of producing postcards. Movies like *The Creature of the Black Lagoon* and *Tarzan Finds a Son* were shot there, highlighting the popularity of the springs and giving people a commercial about just how exotic the place was. It was the promotion that sold the place—beautiful woman under the water promising a dreamland where your normal life washed away. And, of course, there were the monkeys and the wild jungle part of the park that were brought in by a man named Colonel Tooey. This is an attraction that remains a draw and maintains a sense of mystery today.

Many of the people who have worked at the location for a long time will tell you there is something odd about the rhesus monkeys that now roam Silver Springs and the surrounding forests. One ranger said there is something creepy about them and how they move throughout the park, giving an even spookier feel to a place that can be pretty unnerving at night and in the early morning. The ranger said, "I've come up to the docks

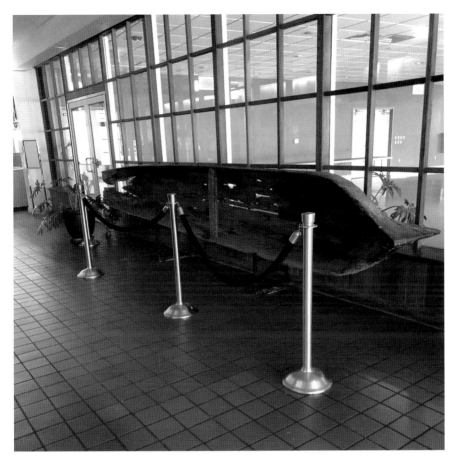

Found deep in the waters of the spring, this boat might have been used by one of the ghostly couples, but its placement in the hall leads many to believe at least one spirit is attached to it.

in the morning and they're just sitting there, staring at me. When I first started working here you could watch the monkeys in the morning diving in the water like they were having belly flop contests. They use the tree to get from one place to another, so you can't keep them in one place." One night, he claims they crashed a promotional movie night the park had set up. The movie was, of course, Disney's *Tarzan*. "There were a whole bunch of monkeys sitting on the grass, just waiting for it to start. I told them they could stay but they need to buy popcorn."

American attitudes and interests changed though, and Silver Springs spent decades trying to find or redefine its identity. Parts were sold off or converted into other things. Buildings were recycled and moved and remodeled. One company bought it, then ABC owned it, then the state took control, then another company and then the state took over again. It was this shuffling of owners and vendors that ultimately doomed the attraction that people had come to love. "Everybody comes in and wants to impress everybody, make it their way, rather than leaving it the way it is," said one old captain.

Wanda echoed his thoughts: "Every concession came in and had their own ideas on how to make money. They build a building to have concerts on, and now it does weddings. They can't keep it straight."

All through the years, though, there have been stories. Whether they are retold to try to rationalize what happens there or just another version of a living commercial, they have offered the park its heartbeat. The beauty of the ghost stories at Silver Springs is that all you need to do is decide what kind of love story you like. They're all tragedies in their own way, but some are more poetic than others.

Take the published account spread by the park itself—at least for a while, until it played itself out. That story involves two young lovers and an old woman who used to work at the park telling the tale. The old woman's name is Aunt Silla, and she knew the young lovers and would sit at the park and tell their story. Claire Douglass was the son of Captain Harding Douglass, a hard man who was tough on those under his command and even tougher on his employees when he took over cotton fields in Florida. He considered it well below their station when his sensitive son fell in love with a beautiful woman named Bernice Mayo. The two had met on the shores of what is now Silver Springs and immediately fell for each other. For quite some time, they walked the banks and traveled on the water and allowed their passion to drown out the protests of his father. Claire eventually promised he would marry her and gave her a family heirloom bracelet until he could get her a real engagement ring.

Captain Douglass found out and shipped Claire to Europe under supervision, hoping he and Bernice would forget each other with the distance. Bernice, who had always leaned on Aunt Silla as a healer and advisor, spent long stretches of time with her, slowly becoming more and more sick. Claire wrote every day, but his father intercepted the letters, and with each day without word back, his lover's health got worse. Eventually, Bernice realized she was going to die. She begged Silla to row her body into the springs to be buried at what came to be called the Bridal Chamber. At first, the old woman disagreed, but when Bernice refused to concede and even went as far as threatening to put a curse on her friend if she did not comply, Aunt Silla promised. That night, under a full moon and with Bernice's dead body on the boat, she rowed out and gently placed the young lady's body in the water. The Bridal Chamber seemed to open up and suck her in.

The next day, the day he had promised to return and marry her, Claire came back and demanded to see his bride-to-be. Eventually, Aunt Silla gave in and rowed the boat to where she had dumped Bernice's body. As he watched the water and cried, Claire saw a hand rise from the rocks with his bracelet on it. He dove into the water and swam down to his beloved, trying to raise her body to the surface. When he realized he could not, he gave in to the water around him and embraced the woman he loved forever.

It has all the elements of a true love story, even if they might be a bit too familiar. For the decades she worked at Silver Springs, Aunt Silla would tell the story, and as the park grew in popularity, it promoted Bernice and Claire's love as part of the attraction, even including it in promotional material. After seeing the enormous snakes and man-eating alligators, you can hop on a glass-bottom boat and see the watery grave and maybe even their ghosts. People talked of seeing lights in the water at night and even a ghostly boat making its way to the Bridal Chamber.

Yet the story is hard to prove, which either adds to its impact or frustrates the listener if you look too closely. There are no birth or death records for Bernice, Claire or Captain Douglass, which is especially odd considering he was supposedly a wealthy man who owned vast amounts of property. The story is presented as true, and Aunt Silla, who was a real woman who worked at the park, solidifies it for the people who remember hearing it.

"Yeah, us older people know that story," said one of the captains who remembers a time when they told the legend while taking people around on the glass-bottom boats. "We don't tell that no more. We discontinued that story long before the state took over. Different ideas with management." With a wink, he will also joke about how people coming in didn't want the ghost part of the story shared with customers anymore either and will also give a little smile if asked whether the water is haunted. He remembers how the story would always change depending on who told it. "Even the captains changed it a little and confused it. That's why you find five different legends out there. Everyone's got their ideas about it. Out with the old, in with the new. We don't tell the other one either."

What other story?

It's hard to tell when the desire for a new story came about and why it was needed, but people shifted away from Bernice and Claire. It might have been because Aunt Silla died or because of one of the many changes

The Twister Palm, where true love can be formed.

in ownership. People who work at the park attribute it to new management and the emphasis on Ross's Seminole Village. The new story was one about Native Americans.

A young man named Navarro from the Tequesta tribe fell in love with a beautiful lady from the Muscogee tribe named Tululah. The tribe's chief, a man by the name of Satouriana, determined that the best course of action would be to send the young brave to the land of the Creeks to report on their power. But there was a bargain made behind Navarro's back, and when he arrived, he was captured and held for more than three months. Tululah was heartbroken and soon grew ill. She eventually died and asked to be buried in the deepest part of the spring, known as the Bridal Chamber. She sunk to the bottom and was engulfed by the rocks. Not long after, her lover returned to hear of her death. He rode out, and the bottom of the Bridal Chamber seemed to open enough for him to see a glimpse of his would-be bride. He jumped from the boat, and as they embraced, the rocks swallowed them. Does that sound familiar?

Though tracking down the real people in the first version is almost impossible, proving this version is false is fairly easy. There is no written record of the tale of Navarro and Tululah until it appeared in the *Ocala Evening Star* in 1907. Its writer, who was on loan from *Talisman*, the newspaper for the Women's College of Florida, which became Florida State University, was Nettie Lisk. Lisk, it seems, was a fiction writer and poet for most of her career, so it is unclear whether she had heard the legend and wrote about it or if she merely created it herself. Also, the tribe identified in the story, the Tequesta, is located more than two hundred miles from Silver Springs. The Muscogee might have been in the area around the time of the founding of the park but not much before then. In fact, the Muscogee are actually part of the Creek, so it seems odd that Navarro would be asked to spy on the tribe that his girlfriend belonged to and that they would then hold him prisoner, especially when there is no evidence that her family opposed the marriage. The legend, however, persists and is said to be the cause of the unexplained activity on the water.

"If you ask any of the rangers who work here at night, they'll tell you that there's something weird in the park at night," said one young employee who has had several of her own ghost experiences in the short time she has worked there. "On the water—they say there are crazy things that happen on the water. If you're here at night, you can feel it."

There might be another story to explain what the rangers see. This one again involves love and is even more tragic and gives parts of the area their names. Ocklawaha fell in love with a beautiful woman named Winona. They were both the children of their tribe's chiefs and thought that revealing their love might lead to war. They instead decided to run away to the Chattahoochee, although there is no tribe by that name. It might instead be a reference to the Chattahoochee River in Georgia. Someone found out about them leaving and decided to stop them. Their pursuer tracked them through the woods and backed the lovers onto a bluff overlooking Silver Springs. Knowing they would be caught and kept apart, they held each other close and jumped from the cliff.

It is said that both sides immediately realized they had made a mistake trying to keep them apart. They named the river that flows into the spring Ocklawaha in his honor and a lake nearby after her. They also say the green moss under the water is Winona's hair. Who is the *they*? It's hard to tell because no one who currently works at the park has ever heard of the two lovers. And there is no bluff that overlooks Silver Springs.

If you haven't had enough of love and suicide, there is yet another story spread by locals and recorded in *Florida Ghost Stories* by Robert R. Jones. This is about another set of lovers—this time named Mourning Dove and Running Fox. For a long time, Silver Springs was called the Peace Camp, and the tribes from near and far would put their differences aside and compete in Olympic-type games. It was there that the two met after Running Fox, who was well known as the best athlete at the games, saved Mourning Dove's life from a poisonous snake. Her heart soured for him, and she took him home to meet her father, who also took an immediate liking to the man. So, the story has a happy ending? Not quite. Another man, Brown Dog, was jealous and angry that Running Fox had beaten him in the races. He struck him with a rock as Running Fox walked the path to visit his new love. As Running Fox lay dying, he put an enchantment on Silver Springs. Anyone who met and fell in love under the "twisted palm" where they had met would be in love forever. When Mourning Dove took his body out to the Bridal Chamber to bury it, she added to what her beloved had said. Anyone who took the flowers from the water and walked with one in each shoe would find love, and putting the flowers in one shoe would get rid of someone who was causing them trouble. She then wrapped a vine around a stone and put it around her neck and threw herself into the water.

Jones goes on to tell another story, which offers some redemption to Brown Dog. Years later, one of the large riverboats was transporting a couple who were to be married in Silver Springs. On one harrowing curve along the way, the woman was thrown overboard, and it is thought that she drowned. When the boat eventually made its way to Silver Springs, those aboard found the woman already there safe and sound. When questioned, she said she had been saved from the water by a Native American who then walked with her to the town. When they reached a certain point, he said he could go no farther and thanked her for allowing him to help. With a good deed

The Bridal Chamber, now known as the Abyss.

done, he had redeemed himself and could move on. She said he had called himself Brown Dog.

These stories are all but lost now. The captains don't tell them, and the young people who work alongside the older ones don't know them. "You just don't have time to talk about them anymore. All of this has changed. We show the people different things and focus on what they want us to. They want to do everything they can to benefit them and forget about the history. They also think there's something maybe upsetting to people now. All that talk of suicide."

Losing the legends is much like the park itself. It is trapped in an in-between time, where a $1 million waterslide stands extinct while the park tries to raise money to maintain the retro façades of many of the attractions. The park is hard to maintain because so much of what made it a place to be back in the day no longer exists to replace the old as it slowly falls apart. Simple things like light fixtures or paint colors are become harder to keep up with as the rarity of the nostalgic pieces becomes greater and money dwindles.

While the legends fade, those who work at the park will tell you it still is one of the most haunted places in Florida. It has been for years. Gina has worked there for most of her life and has seen and felt a ghostly but friendly presence. "There's a ghost in our shop. One of the old maintenance mechanics maybe. I go in there to find something, and I'll hear a noise and turn my head, and there's what I'm looking for. Just enough to turn your head to get to the part." Over the years, this has happened to her quite often, but like many of the people who work at Silver Springs, she understands it's all part of the job.

"The first time I went in there, I was looking for a little copper ferrule. There's this bin with all this copper stuff in there, and I'm looking for one the size of my pinkie. I can't find what I want, so I turn to leave. I hear this chink on the floor. I turned around, and exactly what I needed was on the floor. I said thank you very much." The helper did not stop there and made its presence known again a short time later. "I need another one like a week later and go bopping in there and say, 'Okay Mr. Ghost. What you got.' In the same spot I had picked up the other one, there it is already laying there."

"There is something about the park that is so creepy at night," said Kasey, a newer employee. "There are rangers that live here and say at night there is something that doesn't feel right." For her, the most haunted place on the property is the ballroom. "There's supposed to be a ghost that hangs out on the top floor of the ballroom. I'm not sure of everything that goes on, they just say it's haunted. The managers have their offices upstairs, and they always say they have things happen."

"Everyone here knows it's haunted," she added and told how they share their stories with one another during the slow parts of their shifts, and it did not take her long before she had her own experience. "Work here long enough, and you have something happen. And I haven't even been here long," she said. She was closing up for the night and turned all the lights on the bottom floor off. As she was leaving, all of the lights came back on and then flickered, although there was no one around to play with them.

Her friend Crystal talked about an experience they had together late one night in the ballroom. "We were cleaning in the back, doing dishes. I saw it first, and it didn't move for like five minutes. I was walking in near the window. The lights [from the signs] give it some luminescence. For some reason, I felt something and turned and looked. There was this face. It was floating in the window." Both ladies describe it the same way. They could make out the different features of the face but could not give many details. Both describe it as being there but not there, and for some reason, the ear stands out in their memories.

"I freaked out and ran to get Kasey," said Crystal. "I asked her to go down and look and see if she could see what I saw. She said no because she was terrified. Well, she finally went out there, and she saw it and ran back in to me. Our manager came in, and we asked her if she had seen the face. She said, 'No, what are you talking about?' I walked out, and it was gone."

There is also the breezeway full of displays next to one of the restaurants. Some of the original dioramas created to promote the park were sent to the World's Fair and are featured here, while others are models of the old boats and artifacts from the Seminole Village. Near the entrance is a canoe said to have been pulled from the springs years ago—perhaps the same one used by any of the doomed lovers. According to the whispers Crystal has heard, the displays, especially the boat, cause some unusual activity. "They say there are Native American spirits in that breezeway. They say it's a woman that hangs around there. Between the old village up near the staff parking lot and all the stuff they have in there, it makes sense." She has heard several people talk of the ghosts there and offer the Native American explanation for it. "My boss is sometimes back there late at night, like two o'clock at night. He says he hears that bathroom door open and then slam shut."

Her belief in the spirit was confirmed by a story told by one of the newer workers, who did not know the history of the hall. "The lady went into the female bathroom. It was later in the day. I think it was the back stall that is closed. She said she went in there and the lights started to flicker. She comes out and was washing her hands, and she hears a woman. She turns around, and there was nobody there. She went back to washing her hands, drying her hands. She turns around, and there's an Indian standing there, right where that broken stall is. She ran out of there, and she's never been back. She refuses to go there."

The Bridal Chamber is now known as the Abyss, which might be a fitting name for the place once known for its love stories of sacrifice—not because love is something dark but because it reflects the nature of the legends that once made this a place for lovers. The lore is a deep unknown, set in the middle of a paradise and as inviting for the contrast it creates. The stories are bottomless—never truly dying but swirling around in the water, like Winona's hair, and inviting you to dive in and lose yourself.

8
LOVE AND THE LIGHTS

The Lizzie Borden Bed and Breakfast in Fall River, Massachusetts, is a strange place, and it has little to do with all the reports of ghosts. Lizzie Borden was accused of killing her father and stepmother with an axe in 1892, and in the past few decades, the house where the murders were committed has turned into one of the most haunted spots in the country and one of the most popular paranormal destinations. Between tours and séances and lying on the famous couch where Andrew Borden's body was found, people talk about their experiences with the unknown that have nothing to do with the famous Lizzie. They connect, as if the location itself gives them the freedom to speak about something they normally won't be able to. Then an odd thing began to happen there, and the same thing began to happen at famously haunted places around the country: more and more people were taking dates to the bed-and-breakfast, and parents, usually mothers, were bringing their children as a way to bond with them. The site of a brutal, unsolved murder with a history of paranormal activity had become a place where people showed their love.

The same thing happened years ago in Florida, and while it may not be as famous as it once was, the legend was born of and then fueled by love. Don't look for a clear-cut and easily explained story for the famous ghost lights that appear on a dark patch of road in Central Florida. Science has its say, if you feel comfortable to fall back on that, but it only makes sense if you don't look too carefully. For generations, people have tried to sort out what might cause the lights, and each group that steps forward feels confident that its story

The stretch of road leading into Oviedo.

is best. Looking at all of the legends of the lights, one thing continues to come up time and time again. When we don't know an answer, we fall back on love.

When you have an infamous haunting like the one on Snowhill Road, or Route 13, in Oviedo, what constitutes safety is a matter of when you decide to see it and what story you believe. Known as the Oviedo Lights (in some cases, the Chuluota Lights), they just might be the most well-known paranormal or supernatural story in all of Florida. These simple balls of light, or orbs, have been the subject of speculation, debate and ever-changing folklore for more than 130 years, according to some. Others say they are a more modern creation, usually because it fits their reasoning for the backstory. There is a chance that if you travel on the road to where it intersects with the Econlockhatchee (known to locals as the Eco), you just might witness what has both drawn and terrified generations of onlookers.

Ghost lights might be the most common form of spirit sighting, and what these lights are is largely based on where they are seen. Orbs seen near a cliff are said to be the ghosts of someone who has jumped to their death because of a lost love. Ones seen near water are drowning victims, and the bobbing ball of light near a train track is the lantern of the old switchman who got too close when the train was coming in and lost his head. It might be the setting for the Oviedo Lights that forces people to edit the backstory so often—a dark road in the middle of the night, thick trees hiding a swamp on either side, a bridge going over a fairly innocent river. It is so common and indistinct that people looking to legend trip might miss it. The fact that the location doesn't stand out allows people to attach any story they want to it—a clean slate for what is needed, and it might be the familiarity to many popular urban legends that has allowed some to stick.

The road essentially goes through a swamp. Swamps give off gas that can be ignited and form glowing lights. This happens more in the hot months, partly due to frequent lightning strikes. Science has explained the Oviedo Lights away, but for seven decades, people have not really cared. The logical explanation does not account for the variations of the lights that people see or the personality they seem to have. People are more concerned with the stories, and though the lights can be explained away, the legend still stands up to the potential reality.

For some, it all starts with a lonely soldier coming back from World War II. All through the battles and horrors he saw, one thing kept him going: love. However, when he came back, he found that his love didn't wait for him and fell in love with another man. He walked to the bridge and hanged himself while still wearing his uniform. His soul cannot find rest, so he still wanders on the bridge, waiting for the woman he loved to forgive him and return. It's a story told in some form in locations all over, but is it true? Does it matter for you?

Love sneaks into another popular legend, but this focuses on a mother's love for her children. One night more than one hundred years ago there was a family traveling on Snowhill Road late at night. A thick fog rolled in and made it impossible to see. As they approached the bridge, the driver accidentally drove the carriage off the bridge and into the water below. The mother survived, but three of her children were killed. Her ghost now returns each night to look for her lost children who are also still at the bridge as ghosts, but they can never connect and find peace.

Looking closer at this version of the legend, a few things stand out. The traditional version of the story takes place somewhere else in the town of Oviedo. People see the children walking hand in hand in the field where they died, and the mother is not in the story. Over time, they've escaped their actual death site and made their way to the bridge because the lights were such a popular story and needed an explanation. What the Oviedo Lights actually do points to a tragedy involving more than one ghost, which might be another reason the accident story has taken hold.

While you might see one orb, most people report seeing several. Some have seen them zigzag or act in a playful manner, almost playing hide-and-seek. People walking over the bridge have felt something watching them. They turn to see the lights hovering behind them before zooming off. The lights have been known to follow cars, speeding up when the car does and then mirroring them when they stop. One person reported seeing them fly around the corner like a pair of headlights and then take off into the sky. Parked cars, especially ones where the occupants are getting friendly with each other, can sometimes expect to see the lights come and shine through the windows like a police spotlight. Some have reported seeing them hover over the bridge or gently drift over and through the trees.

October 6, 1969   FuTUre

Can It Kill?

The Oviedo Light

(This is the first in a series of articles which will try to give a reasonable and intellectual explanation for the mysterious light in Oviedo, the light that appears on state road 13. We, on the FuTUre staff, feel that with all the outstanding men and women in the Science departments of Florida Technological University an explanation can and should be found soon.)

This picture was actually taken on State Road 13 by the FuTUre photographer while members of the FuTUre staff witnessed the light.

By Pat Johnson

The road itself gives you an eerie sort of feeling. The reason for this feeling could be explained by the loneliness of the trees on both sides of the road, for the signs of civilization are few. Or it could be caused by the eerie stillness in the area. But, more than likely, the feeling is caused by the ghostly apparition that appears periodically on the road.

The road is State Road 13, in Seminole County just 10 miles from FTU, at an old battered bridge. The apparition is a light, commonly referred to as "The Lights."

Stories of events that happened on state road 13 are numerous and widely circulated, but strangly enough, the reports are only among the so called "younger generation." The majority of adults that were questioned by FuTUre staff members during the initial research for this series either have not heard of an Oviedo light or were to busy to bother with "such foolishness!" A few did have explanations, they called "swamp gas", "just phosphorus", or frequently, "a published parking place for teenagers." The later is to be expected; for it is part of everyday life - where there is a dark road there are parked cars. But if there are couples parked along state road 13, chances are the boy is not taking advantage of the dark night, the location, or the girl - the couple is just sitting, watching, waiting.

They are waiting for the "light" that appears from the vicinity of Snow Hill, a Negro community at the end of the road.

People that have seen the light all agree on its description, it looks like car headlights coming over a hill, but where car headlights seperate and become two, the light in Oviedo remains as one! Some say the light has a blue glow and moves from side to side as it nears the bridge, while others say it's white and moves down the center - but all agree that as it approaches, you are too concerned about leaving to remember its color or the way it moves. 'The light' has never been seen past a certain point of the road. A few years back a group of boys painted a line across the road and tagged it the "Point of No Return". But traffic and age have done away with the line now and only the memory remains.

This faded line is not the only memory shared by 'visitors' to 'the light.' People recall and share tales of:

The cub scouts who were camping in the Oviedo woods when one young scout with a latern mysteriously disappeared forever. Midnight story tellers ask - Could the light be that latern trying to keep others from sharing the young scout's still unknown fate?

The young couple that was found parked on the road one morning with the girl unconscious in the car and her boyfriend's head burned off and mounted on the car like a hood ornament.

The girl who braved the light, and suffered first degree burns on the back of her body, from an unknown source, while running back to her car; in flight of what?

The two boys who were found smothered in their sports car beneath the bridge. No tire marks led to the car. Reason for death: cause unknown!

The boy who was killed playing chicken on the road with the light. A pal was in his darkened car watching the boy as he ran across the street in a race with the invisibly approaching car.

Are these stories fact or fiction? Is there a reasonable explanation for all the events that have been reported on state road 13?

(Next week: Some "Experts" give their opinions.)

Article written in 1969. *Photo courtesy of the* FuTUres *and Pat D'Atrio Johnson.*

No one can agree on an accurate description of the lights, which might also account for why there are so many different legends about them. This is not because people are lying but because there have been so many people who have experienced them over the years. Most have described them as small—between the size of a tennis ball and a grapefruit—although the size might be hard to determine given perspective against a night sky. They are usually said to be greenish blue, but there are also stories of them being yellow white. At times, they are bright and glowing, and other times, they are faint.

There are other stories behind the lights, as well. The lights bouncing through the trees might be responsible for one legend that was popular during the 1990s. There was a young Cub Scout who had gotten separated from his troop that was camping nearby. He got lost in the woods and had a lantern with him that he used to try to signal to his friends, but no one could find him. He was never seen again and might have drowned in the Eco. His ghost returns to the woods to try to find his friends and warn other people to not wander too far.

Then there is the ghost locomotive from the early 1900s. A passenger train from the Florida East Coast Railway went off the tracks, and now the souls of those who died wander the field and the bridge where they lost their lives. In this version, you can see the lights and hear the cries and screams from the victims and a phantom train whistle. An older legend claims that the spirits are Native Americans unsettled by the destruction of their burial mounds in Oviedo itself—forever cursed to wander until their graves are again made sacred.

This is not one of those ghost stories where a few people have seen the lights and then others attach themselves to the story or merely retell what they heard from others. In the 1950s and 1960s, hundreds of people saw them. The lights lay dormant for a while but then had a resurgence in the late 1980s and 1990s and have made another comeback in recent years, when dozens of people have reported them.

The location of the Oviedo Lights has been used as a lovers' lane for more than seven decades, which has helped feed the endless supply of backstories, but it's more than that. Going out to see the lights used to be the hot thing to do. Bored kids from the surrounding towns would pile into cars and make the journey to see them and argue about what they were watching. Men would bring their dates there instead of going to the movies or out to eat, and their dates would be fascinated and maybe a bit terrified by what they were witnessing.

Pat D'Atrio Johnson wrote about the lights in 1969 for the *FuTUres*, the newspaper for Florida Technical University (FTU), now the University of Central Florida. She wrote about how people would come from all around to see them back then—to the point that someone had marked off the best places to stand or park your car to get a glimpse. She also documented how the physics department at the school had held a meeting to determine whether or not the lights were real. While the minutes for that meeting no longer exist, the department did officially come out and say it would look into them seriously if anyone could get a picture.

The FTU physics department seems to be the only one at the college that didn't go to see the lights. The *FuTUres* contains postings and calendars for the university, and it often made references to the legend. Whole groups, including the Art Club, the Math Club and the UFO Study Group, made scheduled trips to see the lights. It was the thing to do. Load up the car, get pizza ahead of time and head out to see the show.

Of course, all who went out there were not necessarily looking for signs of life after death. FTU students joined locals in looking for the lights as a way to find a time and place to be alone with that special someone. Stories of love after death were fueling their passion and were just eerie enough to make dates hold on a little tighter. This gave rise to more variations on the story, which often happens when a local lore catches on and becomes a legend-tripping destination. Couples began to die if they went to see the lights but then decided to spend more time focusing on each other. One story says a couple was making out when the lights came on them. They were too involved to notice. The car exploded, killing them both. Another story tells of a man who left his girlfriend after the shining lights interfered with their night. When he didn't return, she went out to check on him, only to find his severed head on the windshield. His body was never found.

These stories are apocryphal and meant to warn couples to stay away from these kinds of places and keep them from engaging in those kinds of activities, like the famous Hook story. In fact, the severed head is a direct variation of a story often told about the man who leaves the car and is then found hanging from the tree they parked under, with his feet scraping the roof. In a paranormal twist, the dead in these stories become lights themselves, which accounts for why so many people experience them differently. The warnings had very little impact on the spot as a make-out location, though. Couples continued to journey to the bridge to see the lights and park.

On Snowhill Road, it is unclear when most of the stories originated. Like the tale of the couples, legends spark real events, which then spark new legends. For example, more than one story involves the lights running cars off the road. Some of them are the ghosts of those teens who died from being hunted by the balls of light. There has been at least one death in the immediate area, although it may have only been a passing connection to the Oviedo Lights. In 1963, a car was hit by another traveler who had turned out their headlights, and seventeen-year-old Norbert Hyman died. Some attributed his death to someone looking for the orbs. Other deaths and violent incidents have never been substantiated. Hyman's death did cause a general panic in the town and the nearby Florida Technical University about the intentions of the Oviedo Lights, which killed their popularity for a while. People stopped going to see them, but the stories never stopped.

There is something about a haunted location that inspires us to experience it. When people have read enough books or seen enough scary movies, they need to get the next, more intense fix. In recent decades, people have converted old asylums into paranormal playgrounds and advertised hotels as being haunted to attract business. People have bought haunted houses and converted them and sold tickets, scaring people with a mix of backstory and true experiences and a healthy dose of the potential to see a ghost for themselves. These are all late to the show. Central Florida had its own version of a supernatural theme park long before Halloween Horror Nights or the Haunted Mansion. For this one, the ticket is free, and it happens all year long. Just remember to look closely, turn your lights off to get a better view and keep your hands off your date.

9

MARY AND THE DORM

There is a great legend that comes from Venice, Florida, and hits on how a story reveals connections to the community where it takes place. The Ringling Circus would spend most of the year touring the country, but when the winter months approached, it made its way to Florida. Two of the major wintering towns were Venice and Sarasota, but it was not always a happy marriage. Those small communities were tight. They were not without their own scandals and seedier sides, but many locals were hesitant to allow these outsiders in. John Ringling had a brilliant idea. It's said that he paid his employees in only two-dollar bills, with the idea that when store owners counted their money at the end of the day, they would see how many of these bills were in their drawer and know just how much money Ringling's people had given back to the community.

Maybe it's stories like this that have allowed for so much folklore to develop around the man and the places he touched on the Gulf Coast. It could be the mystique around the circus, with its exotic animals seen nowhere else and the vibrant people too intense to be believed performing acts you had never witnessed, but the big top is fertile ground for unexplained stories. Perhaps the best story—the one that truly shows the bond of love between the circus and the communities it eventually called home—is actually a ghostly tale of coming home. It was first written about in Kim Cool's *Haunted Venice* and revolves around one special night a year. For unknown reasons, it is said that the trains carrying the circus and its animals would arrive in town via the Venice Train Depot on Halloween for almost thirty years. People would

Keating Hall on the campus of Ringling College of Art and Design.

come to witness it and cheer. It is now said that every Halloween at midnight the ghostly train can be heard pulling into the station. People have heard the sounds of the whistles and wheels and even the animals roaring and calling from their cars. A few have even seen a spectral train riding on tracks that no longer exist.

The depot is now very different, functioning primarily as a bus station. The tracks that once carried the trains in and out abruptly end, leaving an eerie sense of termination, even during the day. It is, however, in the National Register of Historic Places and runs tours featuring the history of the railways in Southwest Florida. There's a playground for kids to use and a few examples of old trains and memorabilia. At midnight, especially on Halloween, when the unpredictable weather has a habit of causing fog, the old cars and memorials take on a different feeling. They look more like a machine graveyard than a tribute. Much of it, like the statue of animal trainer Gunter Gebel-Williams, is a tribute to the circus that once made the town relevant. Oddly though, no one from the historical society that runs the site or the people working there remembers ever hearing a ghost story about the Venice Train Depot, never mind actually seeing a ghost. It is just another example of the stories that grew up around the circus.

The end of the tracks at the Venice Train Depot.

On the other end of the spectrum, twenty miles away, there is a much different ghost story attached to the infamy of the name Ringling that people have been talking about for nearly one hundred years. While this story might be true, the tale that the students and faculty have been telling about Keating Hall at the Ringling College of Art and Design might be completely wrong. Like most legends, there are secrets and mysteries, and over time, more facts have been added to the truth to make more sense. In this case, the lies might have been spread to cover up an unsolved murder.

It is the story of Mary, but when you take a close look at the story, you might see that her name could really be just about anything. Mary was in love.

The dorm began as a high-end hotel in 1926. Known as the Bay Haven Hotel, it is said to have been one of the nicest places to stay in Sarasota—a city known for its places to stay. It was also reputed to have a seedier side, where some of the upper crust of the city were known to do things that they didn't want the public to know about. Things were not going well for the developer of the hotel's land, though, and in 1928, he died in a car accident. By 1930, the bank owned the building and the attached land, and in 1931, it was bought and became the first building for the new John and Mable Junior College and School of Art. Later, the name was shortened, but the ghost the Ringlings purchased with the hotel has pretty much remained a constant.

It's the kind of love story that haunted houses are made of. Mary is said to have been a prostitute who either lived in the hotel or was known to work out of it. She and one of her clients, supposedly a rich and influential man in the Sarasota business or political scene, fell in love. The man eventually rejected her, some say because he was married and couldn't have an affair become public. Another variation of the story says that she got pregnant. She was so distraught at being thrown aside that she went into the staircase and hanged herself. One version of the story says those stairs were rarely used, and the body was not discovered for some time, maybe not even until the building was sold to Ringling.

Mary might just be the most well-documented ghost in the history of Florida, with the exception of Robert the Doll (explored in the next chapter). She might also be the most frequently seen. Ever since the building became a dorm, people have claimed to see her in the staircase, walking the halls and even in their rooms. She is said to be responsible for turning lights and televisions on and off, locking doors to hapless students and throwing books around the dorm rooms. People have spotted her in mirrors and computer screens and blurry pictures that were focused on something else. She has been the subject of documentaries and student films, and while the core story remains intact, the details have evolved as the students have come and gone.

Descriptions of her seem to point at the possibility of more than one ghost, although no one can say for sure what Mary actually looks like. One description has her as just a skeleton with tattered hair and a ripped dress. While some other students have reported waking up to find this version of the ghost, this seems to be less common. More students have seen the beautiful version, often in a nightgown or stunning dress. One of the common factors in most of the reports is her long, dark hair, which always looks like she just came back from the salon. Mostly, she moves in and out of the shadows, her pale face almost glowing in the dark and her dark lipstick outlining her mouth even when you can't see the rest of her face.

The staircase where Mary supposedly hanged herself.

A former assistant to the president of the college says the reports of the ghost have all but stopped since renovations in 2005 or 2009 and some other alterations to the building over the past few years. Even current students say that Mary is still talked about but not seen. When I talked to her, Julie was a sophomore who did not live in the dorm but had friends who did. "They would tell me the story. I think everyone at the college knows about it, but no one here has actually seen her," she said.

Hauntings can be interesting. When you see a ghost, are you scared because it's not supposed to be there or because it does something to threaten you? Most people say that being in the presence of something they cannot explain is enough, but the stories of Mary run the extremes. Some have said she finds missing objects, especially when they have asked her to help them. She had a habit of locking doors if students forgot to. When most physically saw her, she was just observing them, like she was checking in on their lives and watching the changing world. She often looked sad or worried, making her more pathetic than frightening. Students who experience this side of her have been known to say hello and goodbye to her when they come and go.

Then there are the other sightings where she has appeared hovering over students and floating outside their windows with a menacing look. Some have felt themselves pushed, especially when trespassing on the stairs that have been out of use for a long time. As you would expect, people have seen her decaying body hanging from the third floor before it disappears. One man, Barry, talks of how his friend described to him how he and his buddies were using a spirit board in that staircase. They heard screaming from inside the stairway, even though they were the only ones in there. The board hovered over where her body was found, and then something threw it against the wall.

When it comes to haunted legends, one of the trademarks is a level of consistency. People report the same kind of haunting for years, which is why the backstory makes sense. So many different variations point to one of three things. First, there may be more than one spirit in the building. The hotel did not have the best reputation in the area—golden on the outside but rotten inside. There may have been more than one sketchy thing that happened and more than one death. Due to the infamy of the haunting, it might act as a magnet for other spirits that have passed somewhere else and want to get in on the attention. It would not be the first time that a ghost in one place has been said to draw others to the same location. Second, Mary, for unknown reasons, is moody. She might react to one person very differently than another, perhaps based on what her ghostly wanderings observe about them. It might be possible to be a nice spirit that gets in a bad mood.

The most likely reason is that with such a deep history of a haunting, people are primed to experience things that are not happening or at least to translate those experiences through what they know of the paranormal. Every shadow, every nightmare they wake up from, every odd way the light hits something shiny in the room becomes another example of Mary. This only gets exaggerated when they have to retell the story, changing little details to make people feel the real emotion of the moment and maybe misremembering what happened to them. They have allowed the legend to shape their ideas, and you can cross-reference a list of urban legends with some of the stories being told about the dorm. There are the reports of women having doors locked by Mary against men who are trying to hurt them. Then there are the stories from back in the day that you could conjure her by doing the Ringling version of the Bloody Mary story. Even Barry's board story sounds more like a friend-of-a-friend story than a genuine report. Mary, however, has become such a part of the culture of the school that it might not matter.

Paul Benstine, a paranormal investigator in Southwest Florida, gives another possible reason and explanation about why so many different kinds of ghosts are seen. When he and his team went in to search for the ghost of Mary, they also looked into the structure of the building. By his estimation, the electrical work had worn down over the years, and the wires were emitting enough of an electromagnetic field (EMF) to potentially produce hallucinations. To an investigator, high EMF readings mean a ghost might be nearby, but to an electrician, they mean sickness and delusion. The wiring was replaced during the recent renovations, which might account for why Mary is not seen as much anymore.

Then there is the idea that Mary is not Mary at all. Benstine and his paranormal group, Paranormal Extreme, wanted to do a full investigation of the location and went on a deep dive to see if they could track down who Mary really was and if she had died the way it was reported. After contacting historical societies and looking over official Sarasota records, they created a profile. They had a time frame, an area she had died in and an estimated age. They found the name Minnie Belle Hughes, a Black woman who was born in Miami but was known to have moved to Sarasota. Her death certificate lists her profession as "undresser," which was a euphemism used in those times for a prostitute. It claims that she died of food poisoning.

Then the research got even more bizarre. Minnie is not buried where the death certificate and the records say she is. This might be explained away. Perhaps they did not know where her resting place would be and assumed that she would be interred at the primary African American cemetery in the city. However, no one knows where her body actually is. Extensive research has not been able to locate where it went after leaving the hospital. Furthermore, the death certificate itself has been tampered

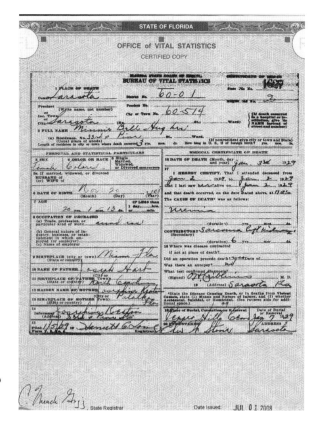

The death certificate of Minnie Belle Hughes. *Photo courtesy of Paul Benstine and Paranormal Extreme.*

with. The writing is clearly in two different pens, one of which is ballpoint, which was not in use at the time of her death. The undertaker who signed the death certificate actually died six years before he signed it, and the other died mysteriously not long after.

All of this, Benstine believes, points to a coverup. Minnie must have been sleeping with someone powerful in the town. There might also be truth to the pregnancy aspect of the story, although that is not in the autopsy. Benstine believes the most likely story is that she was murdered in the stairs and didn't kill herself. He believes that her body was removed before the police were called. Part of his confirmation comes from the investigation Paranormal Extreme did in the staircase. The group was in the middle of its research when it was allowed in with college supervision. At one point, an unseen voice said the full name of Minnie Belle Hughes on one of the recordings they got. When the investigation took place, they had not yet fully looked into her history, and the college officials who supervised the time in the stairwell were mystified when they heard the voice.

The mystery of who Mary is might never be solved, and the students at the school might not even care. She has become a sort of mascot for them—something that people pass down to freshmen and talk about come Halloween. Like many hauntings, the details overshadow the story behind them. The students might reference it, but the real lore is when she pops up and scares you or moves something in your room. They forget the story began with a woman in love who had things go the wrong way.

10
TWO CASES OF OBSESSION IN KEY WEST

Peaople either love or hate Key West—it has that kind of polarizing effect on the people who visit. Some are turned off by the crowded streets and bars, the public drinking and crooked roads that are not nearly as interesting as their friends talked about. Those who love it are drawn to it and spend their time away thinking about getting back to island time. There's something romantic about a place so close to its history, with buildings dating as early as just about anywhere in Florida's history but mixed with a modern touch of art. Every night, people gather to share a moment as the sun sets on Mile 0, knowing they may never see any of the people around them again but that they have shared a singular experience, repeated night after night but individual at that moment.

There is another face to Key West that the people there know about that they don't often share with the tourists. It's just below the surface, like Hemingway puffing out his chest while dealing with depression or clean streets after Hurricane Irma hiding alleys where the debris was stacked up. That's the other side of obsession—one eye too focused and the other one blind. Some believe Key West is cursed. The great thing about curses is that the idea comes after bad things have happened, making it hard to separate the cause from the effect and having all possible tragedies comfortably link to the same root. Key West is an example of a place that naturally lends itself to the unfortunate events that have happened to it, but given a story here and a legend there, the natural becomes supernatural. The fact that Key

West is still standing, rebuilding itself while remaining true to its history and color each time, is a legend in itself.

It's impossible to say *ghost* and *Key West* and not talk about the doll, and he's a great example of the two sides of his hometown. In a land of fantasy and legend, Robert the Doll stands out and has been one of its paranormal superstars. People flock from around the country to see the haunted toy encased in plastic and decorated with letters from people who went to see him and needed to share their experiences. There's an industry built around him, fueling ghost tours, merchandise and multiple television appearances. Most people, drunk with Robert fever, gloss over the darker elements

Robert the Doll.

of his backstory and focus on the creepiness of a haunted doll known to pull pranks and mess with the people who visit. They do not understand how one boy's love may have led to a man's obsession, which may have led to the creation of a fiend.

The legend, and there are many versions, tells of a housekeeper who had made a three-foot doll for little Robert Eugene Otto, who went by the nickname Gene. The real story may be more mundane. He may have been a gift after a business trip overseas or sewn together by a neighbor. Either way, Gene named the doll Robert and dressed him in his own clothes. The most popular of the legends tells of the housekeeper being fired and placing a curse on the doll before she left, although this tends to be a newer aspect of the story. The curse might have been created by the attention Gene gave the doll because it's said that he went everywhere with it and spent all of his time playing with and talking to it. Then something odd began to happen. Gene's parents and people working in the house often heard an odd voice responding to him when he talked to Robert. Unexplained things would happen in the house in rooms that were seemingly unoccupied. Things would crash or go missing, and people couldn't open doors that had no locks. Gene would respond with what become his catchphrase: "Robert did it."

As time went on, the incidents got worse, and Gene always claimed it was the doll who had done the bad act. Things didn't change when he got older and married. He kept the doll and fussed over him, often taking

Haunted Key West Lighthouse.

him for walks in the neighborhood. Objects continued to move on their own, and whispers kept being heard throughout the house. Gene's wife demanded that he move the doll to the attic, although that did little to curb the activity. Eventually, Gene died. One of the stories states that Gene was found in the attic with Robert on top of him, and Robert remained when the property switched hands. By then, his popularity had started to rise. Eventually, Robert was moved to the East Martello Museum on the edge of Key West, where he remains today, although he is sometimes taken out and toured around the Keys or brought to conferences.

Now people who visit are forced to follow Robert's Rules when visiting him: say hello when you arrive, say goodbye when you leave and don't take a picture without asking. Those who don't ask risk having their pictures not come out. Even worse, the room is filled with firsthand accounts of people who did not follow the rules and lost their luggage right after. Some missed planes or got into car accidents after being disrespectful, while others attribute sicknesses and even death to their visit.

Often ignored in the Robert story is the story of Gene. Was it a case of an eccentric artist, or was there something darker at work? Was it a curse, or did his fixation on Robert actually lead him to create a ghost?

Lost in the shadow of the doll is a very different case of love turned to obsession. Lighthouses are meant to be beacons—something in the darkness meant to guide you to safety. The Key West Lighthouse did its job for more than one hundred years, surviving natural disasters and physical changes to light the way into Key West. That is not where its story ends, though. Lighthouses are also symbols of isolation and dedication to duty—places where the loneness of the job can breed fierce loyalty and unhealthy focus. Like Key West itself, there are two faces to the tower, and the same guiding light that brought ships safely into harbor might have been a magnet to many of the restless spirits still remaining on the island. More importantly, it may have been one woman's passion that provided the spark.

Like many ghost stories in Florida, this one might have started with the Spanish. On arriving in what is now Key West, they unearthed burial mounds and ignored the holy site in favor of an outpost. They found enough bodies to call the new territory Caya Hueso, or Bone Island. When Florida switched hands to the United States years later, they wanted to use it as a naval base and needed a lighthouse to support it. Almost as soon as it was commissioned, there was mystery behind it. The base was almost abandoned due to disease. The first man sent to look after the construction of the lighthouse in 1824 left Boston with men and materials and was never seen again. The construction

The grounds of the lighthouse and museum, said to be haunted by any number of ghosts.

suffered delay after delay, perhaps due to the conditions of the location or perhaps due to the curse. Over the years, the lighthouse, as well as the base and fort it supported, would suffer one misfortune after another. Violent storms, yellow fever and leprosy and personal tragedy would find their way there. People wrote letters home telling of the horrors of living there, and rumors had already started about the dead coming back to life to torture those who had lived.

Yet this is really a story of a woman. Barbara Mabrity came with her husband and children to run the lighthouse on its opening in 1826, when he was made its first keeper. Michael Mabrity was dutiful to his mission, but six years later, he died of yellow fever. Barbara took over. Every description of the woman paints her as a tough, strong-headed woman who made her life running and managing the grounds with her children in tow. During her time, she ushered the town through several hurricanes, the worst of which happened in 1864. The Havana Hurricane blew in and wreaked havoc on Key West, destroying the Sand Key Lighthouse and tumbling the Key West Lighthouse. More than a dozen people had gone to the lighthouse for shelter, and when it was destroyed, Mabrity was only able to save one of her children. The rest perished along with the others inside. While this story has been told for years, research suggests it is only a legend, as several of her children went on to run the lighthouse after her death. She was eventually fired for speaking out against the government during the Civil War, in 1864, but she never quite got over the routine that had been her life for forty years.

Over the years, the lighthouse has changed. After the storm, it was rebuilt, and until it was decommissioned in 1969, it was constantly modified, from using whale oil to electronics. One thing has not changed, though. Barbara Mabrity still comes to work. For more than one hundred years, people have talked of seeing a female figure climbing the stairs to the top of the tower and then disappearing. Paranormal experts call this kind of haunting a residual haunting—someone repeating the same action of climbing eighty-eight steps for years after the person is no longer there.

The Artist's House—Robert's former haunt.

There is, however, more to her ghost. Others have reported her in the courtyard at the base of the tower and where the keeper's quarters have been turned into a museum. There are even sightings of a woman said to be Barbara on the edge of the water still waiting for the next storm to test her will and the strength of her lighthouse.

Even though there are pictures of Barbara from when she was alive, some witnesses could be confused. There are said to be more ghosts on the grounds of the lighthouse than places in Key West that serve key lime pie. It's as if the lighthouse is also a beacon for the ghost nearby. While Key West has a ghost in just about every building, the grounds of the lighthouse are where many walk and talk. People have reported phantom couples who disappear, a man who looks disoriented and vanishes when approached and small children playing. There are people in military uniform and a black mist that comes and goes, mostly at sunset.

The list of potential suspects makes it difficult to determine who these spirits might be. Legend says the children are Barbara's— or at least children who died during the Havana Hurricane. There were outbreaks of yellow fever throughout the 1800s, causing dozens of deaths near the tower. It is said that one of Barbara's children, Mary, who grew up and ran the lighthouse, suffered the disease herself. She and her husband, who also died of yellow fever, walk together on the property. Other legends tell of the Native American curse. The souls are those who were disturbed when the Spanish arrived, or those who died in the area are forced to remain near the lighthouse as payment for destroying the graves.

Obsession can be a dangerous thing. It blinds us to what true reality is and allows rose-colored glasses to change our perspective. Making a connection to something, whether it is a special toy like a doll or what you do for a living, is an important part of discovering something to be passionate about. Obsession takes it too far, focusing intent and intentions and making the object of our affection a prison. It can be the dark side of love and, in some cases, might keep us going back to something, refusing to let go, even when we should have moved on. Instead of love, that sounds like the beginning of a ghost story.

11
Mini-Lights, Mini-Lights, Come Out Tonight

Tonight, go to Booker Creek in St. Petersburg, Florida. Lean over the edge and look at the water, which appears more like the dirty, foamy stream at the end of your driveway when you wash your car than a waterway. Hold your breath for a moment, close your eyes and say, "Mini-Lights, Mini-Lights, come out tonight" three times. Try not to notice that noise behind you as you finish. But then the rustling will get louder and will come from all around you. You'll see a glowing figure a bit away from you, moving quickly as it runs the distance between the two of you. You'll turn to escape, but a pair of pale blue hands—too strong for how small they are—will grab your leg and won't let go. The other figure will get closer. You're in an urban neighborhood. Tropicana Field is only a few miles away, but you're alone, and you know, because you've heard the stories for years, that you might never be seen again.

Here's the thing about urban legends and folklore: they're always in the background and ready when you need them. They sit on the shelf with all of their universal truths waiting for moments when they make sense to a community or something needs to be explained. The right situation, the right necessity, and they'll jump out like memories with springs on them and fill the void. They make sense because you've heard them before, but you also nod your head because something is missing, and logic can't tell you why.

The story of the Mini-Lights is one that keeps changing and adapting to its environment—a sign of the times. It's nearly impossible to create a straight narrative line that tells the whole story of them because everyone

The Mini-Lights are said to be on different bridges throughout Booker Creek.

has their own line. Over the years, the tales have been twisted and combined and borrowed and cut so that everyone who talks about them tells their own version. That makes a folklorist smile, but it leaves a storyteller struggling to choose how to start the story the right way. What's the "in" story, and how do you weave it the right way? No one can even agree on what they should be called: Minnie Lights, Mini-Lights, Mystery Lights, Midget Lights, Minnie's Lightning, Mini Lightning, Merry Lights or the Mennonites.

It might be best to start the story with a description of what people have physically claimed to see or, more accurately, what they claim other people have told them they see. Firsthand sightings are almost nonexistent nowadays. People state that they have witnessed or heard stories of two strange, almost monstrous, small people around a bridge or in a field near the bridge in one of three possible locations in St. Petersburg. Descriptions vary about what is seen. An article in the *Tampa Bay Times* says the creatures are "bluish-greenish-gray, bald and small." Some say they are small people whose skin has a green or pale glow to it. Other people say they are just dressed in all green with painted skin but have glowing green or red eyes. Stories are out there saying they are more like ogres. In modern times, people have said the Mini-Lights are now dead and exist as ghost lights of white and green and blue nearly as large as a small child, floating or seeming to run at you.

Both the people and the orbs are said to appear and disappear at will, popping up and seeming to surround you, supporting the idea that they are paranormal or undead sewer travelers. The most important aspect of their behavior, and the one that both inspires their infamy and explains it, is that they abduct people and take them away, never to be seen again. They may physically attack you or try to intimidate you to get you to leave, but it is likely that if you see them, it's too late. There will be no evidence left behind.

The legend is said to date back generations but has experienced a resurgence in the last few years, partly due to the nearby baseball team and partly due to a new movie made about them. When newspapers mention them, they get responses from readers who all know the details, as they were told by sources, and when Facebook and social media posts go out asking residents for their versions, there is always an avalanche of creepy and often conflicting descriptions. The legend also has a significant racial element to it and seems to be spread more in the African American community of the city. While adults have been said to be attacked by the Mini-Lights, it is primarily a story that offers a warning to children and young adults, which might be the reason it has existed for so long. Kids always need a little extra to keep them scared enough to do what's right.

It is a story of outsiders and the fear we have of them. The origins of the folklore often begin with a person outside of the community who the people need to be protected from. In the neighborhoods where the lore has taken hold, this is often a racial conflict. Every time the story gets passed around, it has something to do with gentrification, the changing of the community to fit the needs of the outsider, whether it is the destruction of homes for development in the 1920s and 1930s or the construction of the baseball field and the switching over of local businesses to ones catering to fans.

We can start with the witch because she is somewhat consistent to the story. She lived in a shack near Booker Creek and was named Minnie. At times, she is said to have resided under a bridge that crosses the creek. No one is sure of when she lived there or how she came to the area, but she was protective of her land. Anyone approaching would soon find themselves being chased off by two protectors. Some of the stories claim that these were her sons or maybe even circus freaks she worked with while she was with the circus herself. Others claim they were monsters she had captured or even a witch's familiar, maybe born of some horrible spell that mutated humans.

Minnie has also been said to be a Mennonite, a member of a religious group who would have been considered an outsider at the time. Misunderstandings caused people to mistrust and shun her, sometimes going as far as vandalizing her property. Another version of the story says she allowed circus performers to stay with her, which angered people who did not want them in the community. They attacked, and her visitors would protect her.

As the area developed, they say the shack was torn down and Minnie disappeared, perhaps leaving a curse on the area. Another tale says she was upset when she had to give up part of her land when builders began developing and sought her revenge. Others say she left, but for a while, the shack remained, and you could conjure something by circling her house and chanting her name. In some stories, the house is a Mennonite church near the bridge, or she is a Mennonite who moved into an abandoned Christian church. Either way, Minnie is long gone, but the little ones remained in the area, perhaps as ghosts, and still wander around at night. They can be brought out by calling out, "Mini-Lights, Mini-Lights, come out tonight" three times at a specific place near the water.

Here's where things get a bit more confusing, if you aren't confused yet. There are several locales people associate with the story. Online and news sources retell it as happening at very specific locations and addresses. Most of them focus on one of three spots all connected to Booker Creek: Roser Park, Thrill Hill and Childs Park. All three are well known in the area and are places where parents look to keep their kids safe.

Thrill Hill gets its name from the steep climb and quick drop of the road as the bridge crosses over the creek. The legend may be closely tied to the slow loss of the community. If you take a trip there, you will notice the streets alternating between close-together, rundown houses and large, well-kept properties. Thrill Hill itself is more of an industrial park, with large businesses and docks on either side—most fairly new to the area. It is a place where business has cut into community. It is also a place where a child could easily get hit by a car coming down the drop. If the Mini-Lights are a warning, this would be an ideal place to have kids avoid.

One of the images in stone at Thrill Hill.

Of all three locations, this is the only one that had enough water to support a boat and a large enough space to lend credence to the living-under-the-bridge aspects of the story. The neighborhood, however, is far from spooky. Cars fly by constantly, and the lights and music from nearby businesses break any creepy atmosphere that might have been there at some point. It seems more likely that parents wanted to keep their kids safe and may have borrowed the legend to keep them off the street at night.

Roser Park is the most popular setting for the story. The area is 270 acres and has almost 150 historic homes, some of which are beautiful estates, while others have the same rundown look as some of the tougher sections of the city. The main path that cuts through it is lined with houses and markers telling of the history, development and renaissance of the neighborhood. Just past the trees and bridge crossings are several hospitals, the main one of which is Johns Hopkins Children's Hospital. While the hospital is considered an important part of the community, it cuts into what used to be neighborhoods, and its construction, much like that of Tropicana Field, forced many families to leave the area.

The bridges at Roser Park are much smaller and cross Booker Creek at several places. There is one spot, however, where the creek takes a turn. It also has a field nearby that fits the description of how the monsters would cover an expanse of land chasing you down. The multiple crossings could also account for the Mini Lights seeming to appear and disappear if they traveled through the water and could jump up from anywhere. If the story's really a tale of progress cutting into a neighborhood, this would make a perfect location.

The last place is a perfect setting for a horror movie. The Mini-Lights have always been about keeping children safe, so where better to warn them than Childs Park, a playground on Booker Creek. Many of the modern newspaper references come from this site, and there are elements of the story that can only take place here. There is a random cement foundation, which might have been the place where Minnie's house once stood or at least inspired that part of the story. It is situated near a large entrance to the sewer that could have been where her foot soldiers could move throughout the area and create the impression that they could appear and disappear at will. Spend time there at night, and you'll hear noises coming from the tunnel.

Location two, Roser Park.

Childs Park, another
suspect for the Mini-Lights.

They are probably not little green men trying to take you away, but they are something that may act as a major element of why the legend exists.

Researchers, including Mark Muncy in his book *Creepy Florida*, discovered a possible twist to the backstory that is even more frightening than monsters or ghosts. Alligator farms used to be big business in Florida, as you can tell from the number of alligator attractions that still exist and the volume of legends that involve bringing baby alligators home that then roam free in the sewers of every major city. The story goes that Black children were kidnapped to work on these farms. They would feed the alligators because the actual workers didn't want to risk the danger, and the kids would often be eaten by the animals. Some of the more horrific stories tell of them being fed to the alligators intentionally, sometimes in front of cheering crowds. If you need proof that this may have happened, you need only to look at some of the advertisements and memorabilia for those farms back then that show the beasts going after little Black children. One even has the kid in his mouth. While this may just be a legend to explain the legend, there was enough concern about it for parents to warn their kids to avoid the streets at night to keep from being taken. There was even concern that alligators in Booker Creek, especially where the tunnel is at Childs Park, were the

The entrance to the waterway and a home for Mini-Lights and alligators.

ancestors of those animals who had been set free or escaped the farm and had a preference for eating Black children.

Abduction might also be at the root of another potential element of the lore. Sometime between 1912 and 1914, George and Willie Muse were working in the fields near their home in Truevine, Virginia, not far from Roanoke. As detailed in the book *Truevine* by author Beth Macy, a "freak hunter" named James Herman "Candy" Shelton saw them and kidnapped them. The African American brothers both had albinism, and Shelton knew he could sell them as a sideshow attraction, maybe even to one of the big circuses like Ringling. They spent the next thirteen years as Eko and Iko, a featured attraction, billed as everything from aliens to monsters to cannibals from deep within the jungles of Africa. They were big business and brought in even more money when they actually did become part of Ringling. In 1927, they returned to Roanoke to perform. That was where their mother, Harriet, saw them and knew at once that they were the children who she had never given up hope of finding. For the next few years, she fought to get them back and out from under the circus's thumb.

The brothers loosely match the description of the Mini-Lights when they had physical bodies, especially with their white skin and the dreadlocks they

101

were forced to grow to make them appear even stranger and more exotic to White audiences. The story was told as a cautionary tale in Virginia and some of the surrounding states for a while—be careful of people from the circus or you'll be the next Eko and Iko. While some sociologists claim this was more of a regional story, the connection to the circus cannot be overlooked. Ringling is an important influence in that part of Florida, and many of the variants of the Mini-Lights legend involve circus people. After being set free, the brothers continued to be paid to perform for Ringling, making them known in the area. In fact, they were in court in Orlando in 1928 because they had continued to perform without the consent of their guardian and manager, Shelton. All of this was going on as the Mini-Lights story was gaining more traction in the community just an hour or so to the west.

If a legend doesn't fit, feel free to change it up. If a ghost story doesn't make sense, if it's questioned by the audience, it is okay to add a detail here and there so that listeners understand the basic meaning. Truth just makes things confusing. In the Booker Creek neighborhood, the story is always in flux, much like the city is always in flux. Head out to the bridge. There might be an ogre or a monster or a ghost out to get you. You may be hunted by a witch or an alligator or someone looking to make you part of the circus. All of the stories are true because they resonate with someone, and if you don't like the one you hear, you can pick from the salad bar of another to connect to it. One thing is certain though: when you're in St. Petersburg, avoid bridges and saying anything three times.

12

THE GHOSTS PROTECTING SAFETY HARBOR

This is really the story of two men separated by hundreds of years and brought to the same site for different reasons. One is nameless, identified only by his job title and his importance to the people who surrounded him. The other is well known—sometimes more myth than man and veiled in mystery. It is also the story of a place that meant something specific to each man involved and proves worthy of revisiting and protecting. The ultimate sign of love is to be willing to sacrifice yourself for the thing you have a passion for—to stand guard when that thing is in danger and to risk your own life to keep it safe. Safety Harbor is one of those places. Tucked away in another world, far from the twin ports of Tampa and St. Petersburg, it's like stepping back in time when you've grown accustomed to city life.

This is also the story of a monster, but not the kind that you usually hear about.

It starts with a legend told by people in Florida about various parts of the state. Whether it's the Florida Keys or Miami or a place like Tampa, there is a belief that some cities and towns across the state are protected from the storms that ravage others. When hurricanes hit, and they have hit often, something protects these communities from harm, even going back to the old tribes of Florida. Logic might say that people merely settled where the storms were less known to hit or that survivors tell the history of a place. However, anyone who has spent time staring at a spaghetti map before a major storm, hoping that their town gets spared, can tell you that

The Temple Mound at Philippe Park.

there is an unpredictability that dominates the movement of this kind of weather. Depending on who you speak to, they are saved because those places are sacred and protected by spirits. Whether it was through prayer or sacrifice, the storms, which were thought to be living breathing things by Native Americans, could be bargained with and knew to leave certain places alone.

At Safety Harbor, it goes one step further. There, the legend says a shaman was responsible for the protection of the people. It was the land of the Tocobaga—their capital if you believe the archaeologists who have discovered evidence that it existed for more than one thousand years. The focus of the village, which was more like a city with more than five thousand people, was the Temple Mound, where the shaman lived and would conduct rituals. Originally rectangular, it was the primary social spot as well, with the rest of the people set in smaller settlements and houses around it. In Safety Harbor, the Temple Mound was on the water, so the rest of the people lived on the other three sides. Like most of the tribes in Florida, the Tocobaga were mound builders, so in addition to one being the main worship location, there would have been others, including burial mounds, throughout.

The shaman's primary responsibility was to keep the people safe, and given the strategic location of the village and the mound, he would have been able to spot invaders and other threats. He could also predict the weather from that height. The stability of the settlement was based on his ability to summon a great monster, also known as a Spirit of the Earth, to fight anything that might attack. Legend says the shaman would raise it, and the creature would fight a battle with the beasts from the sea and the Spirit of the Wind. Sometimes it would beat them back completely, and other times, it would do enough damage to keep the destruction of the village to a minimum. They were never completely untouched by the storms, but the monster would always do enough to keep them safer than their neighbors.

The story was known enough that other tribes would ask for protection from the Great Spirit. It was also feared enough that people thought twice before they attacked. Only the shaman could call the spirit, so he not only held an honored place among the people but also had to choose who he would pass the information to before he died. The stories also say the last shaman died before he could fully pass the skill to the next generation, and because of this, he must continue to protect the land he loved in death.

Today, the Temple Mound is part of Philippe Park in Safety Harbor. The village is gone, replaced by picnic tables and walking trails. The mound itself remains in a smaller form, now more of a pyramid than a rectangle, but the other mounds have been unearthed and removed. There is a paved walkway to the top on its north side, and on the other three sides, there is concrete and beautiful masonry stairs that weave from the base to the top. While not entirely honoring its original form, there is something respectful about how the final remaining mound is treated. Most people who spend time

View from the top of the mound.

there might not know the full importance of the location, but many who do understand know the ghost stories associated with it.

A shadowy figure is often seen climbing the mound from the west side at dusk. Most believe he is the last shaman making his way to the top to replay his old ceremonies and perform his old duties. There is a different feel to that side of the mound—an electricity and an odd atmosphere that people report when they spend time in the park. He is seen at all times of the year, most often during the three days surrounding the full moon, and is said to predict coming storms when he climbs to summon the spirit to protect his beloved land. This is why the town is known as Safety Harbor and why Tampa has a reputation of being one of those hurricane safe zones.

There might be more than just the shaman who returns to worship at the mound. People have seen other figures on the west side during twilight. Some have reported full apparitions while others have seen lights crossing the field and rising up the hill. Others talk of an odd disturbance in the air, like seeing heat rising off pavement in the form of a man, in the same location. These might be the spirits who were disturbed when the burial mounds were destroyed. According to recreations of Tocobaga villages, these fields were where burial mounds would have been located. The spirits might also be traveling to worship—the followers of the shaman still respecting the man who protected them and their families.

When people can actually see them, these spirits are always referred to as being Native Americans in features and clothing—except for one of them. There is another ghost who continues to return to the place he stood to protect his family. Why he still walks the grounds of his old home is the subject of debate among the people of the town.

Depending on what history you want to believe, Count Odet Philippe is either a founding father or a slave-owning con man. Chances are, like most figures in history, he's both, but they say his ghost is a little more straightforward. He is seen in different parts of the park, mainly near the Temple Mound, and people think it is him because of his love for the land and the fact he is the only spirit who doesn't look like a Tocobaga. He is mainly seen on the paved path that leads to the mound and is captured as only quick glimpses or a solid figure who fades quickly when noticed. There is something that keeps him in that place, and the clue might be in his long history with the area.

Born in Lyon, France, in 1787, Philippe came to America via Charleston, South Carolina, in 1822, on the heels of some potentially sketchy business dealing in his home country. Claiming to be a doctor, he made his way to

A view of the west side, where people are said to climb to the top of the Temple Mound.

Key West in 1836 and was able to amass a small fortune. This has led to speculation that he became deeply involved in the slave trade there and benefitted from illegal dealings with the Cubans and the Spanish. When the United States government was looking to develop more land on the Gulf for protection after the Seminole Wars, he accepted 165 acres and quickly went forward developing a plantation.

He created a homestead, legend says, near the Temple Mound and began working the land, perhaps with his own slaves, tearing through the land and destroying the other mounds as he went. Most of this is rumor, but it's worth noting that the landscape changed after his arrival, so it can only be assumed the sacred site's annihilation was due to his development. Over the next few years, he changed the economy of Florida itself, introducing the grapefruit to the state and bringing cigar making to the Gulf and making it one of the leaders in the industry in the States.

Why he might be left on the land is as hard to pin down as what kind of person he really was. The first legend says that he is cursed by the people whose own death he disturbed. He is forced to walk the grounds until they are all returned, and he must go to the Temple Mound to ask forgiveness of the shaman there. The other has to do with his connection to the Great Spirit that once saved his life. During a hurricane in 1848, his plantation and homestead was miraculously saved after he went to the mound to seek shelter. Damage was done to most of the buildings in the area, but the violent storm stayed mostly clear of Helena, the name he had given his land. While some believe it was just the beast doing his job or even the work of the shaman, some say Philippe had heard the old stories and made some kind of deal. His continued presence on the land is part of that deal.

It may even be some karma from the universe that keeps him at Helena. Like the many bodies he might have displaced in his time there, no one is quite sure where he is buried. While there is a clear marker for him, people believe the original headstone was destroyed and his body lost. This is an odd and unconfirmed aspect of the story, though. There are several pictures of schoolchildren visiting the grave during ceremonies and school field trips, so to say they did not know where the body was doesn't fit with the historical evidence. These trips were only a few years ago, not generations ago, so it seems a bit like part of the mound legend finding its way into his story. That said, the path where his ghost is seen begins directly across the street from his marker and connects to the base of the mound.

When looking at the unexplained, no culture's folklore should be overlooked, so there is another weird spiritual connection to the land at Philippe Park. There is an unusual number of trees that have the appearance of traditional fairy trees. According to descriptions as old as the Tocobaga legend but originating in Europe, these can be identified by their holes and hollow sections, which are often explained away by disease or animals. These are said to be planted or built by the fairies themselves or transformed for their use and act as gateways between worlds for spirits and other

Left: Odet Philippe's grave marker but not where he is buried.

Right: One of the many potential fairy trees that circle the Temple Mound.

supernatural creatures to travel through. While the Temple Mound used to be surrounded by smaller mounds and houses, these trees now form almost a semicircle around it. Their planting would be around the time of Philippe or after, which means many of them are rooted in the soul, where the tribe's bodies once laid, and may act as a doorway for them to return to the Temple Mound. One is even built right into the mound, with the staircase twisting around it to preserve it.

Home is the place where you are supposed to feel safe. It's where we go when everything else is unsure or unstable to find our center and connect with those we love. If life is a storm, home is the umbrella, the safe harbor to breathe and relax before taking on the world again. Ghosts are supposed to do the opposite for us. They disturb the peace and make us feel unsafe and unwelcome. That's not the way the story goes in Safety Harbor. There the ghosts are looking after you like you're one of the family and making sure you're tucked in safe before the storm hits.

13

THERE ARE TOO MANY LOVE STORIES AT INDIAN SPRINGS CEMETERY

A good ghost story starts with a strong backstory. It's fine if there's a shadowy figure or a disembodied voice calling your name. Those things scare us because they're not supposed to happen. They disrupt the order we love and what we expect to happen. A cemetery is supposed to be scary, so it has an unfair advantage if you're looking to experience something eerie. No backstory is needed. Things get even odder if there is a backstory, though, and the more you can go back and check on the rumors between the rows, the creepier the place gets. When you can relate to the story, like let's say a love triangle or a mother missing her children or a man who died doing the job he loved, just stepping in is enough of a scare.

The trouble with Indian Springs Cemetery in Punta Gorda is not the backstory of the ghosts that people see there. The trouble is trying to pick which ghost visitors are actually encountering. An entire cast of characters is laid to rest there in mystery and buried with secrets they may still carry. Waking among the headstones is like taking a tour of the history of Charlotte County, and looking into the past of the players is like following a tree where the branches twist and come together and then rise up somewhere else to grow along another limb. If every cemetery is a history book waiting to be opened, Indian Springs is a murder mystery and may be one of the oldest whodunits in Southwest Florida.

If you've ever heard of a local haunted cemetery and what happens there, then you have a handle on the paranormal activity at Indian Springs. It has

Indian Springs in Punta Gorda, the home to more than one ghostly love story.

become a popular stopping point for paranormal investigators in the area because it has so much unexplained activity and a deep and documented reputation. People often feel like they are being watched when they go there during the day, and many have felt something tapping them in the small of their back or tugging at their leg. Odd lights, including orbs, are frequently seen at night. Figures are said to walk around after dusk, and whispers are heard in the older section of the cemetery. One couple reported seeing a young man and woman bending over, appearing to read a headstone and then dissolving away. Other parts of the cemetery are like entering a vacuum—all outside noises stop. One section contains only children, and at night, people say you can hear the children laughing and playing and even see them running between the graves. A tall, shadowy figure has been seen in that section as well. The most popular legend is that of a scream heard in one section. While no one is quite sure who it is, the voice has been reported by dozens of people over the years.

When you research the history of any small town, you'll always find connections between the people there, so it is easy to see conspiracy theories with every turn. Looking at the past makes your vision better. Punta Gorda is not unique in this, but there is almost a folklore perspective on its history that forms in the neighborhoods of small communities, especially when newcomers push on all sides. Everything is well documented, but people believe there is so much more between the lines to the point that the rumors of what has happened are as much a part of the times gone by as the written word.

Would you want to be buried near the person who killed you, for example? Marshal John Bowman is said to be one of the spirits seen at night. Brought in to help clean up the bootlegging and corruption of the town, he was the type of lawman one might envision in the Old West and not a town carved out of a swamp. Given his thick mustache and piercing eyes, you can imagine lesser men melting as he interrogated them or laid his enormous hands on them to take down a criminal. From all accounts, he was successful in bringing some level of law to a town facing heavy corruption and behind-the-scenes lawbreaking. He was so successful, in fact, that in 1903, he was assassinated by a gunman who shot him through his window as he held several of his children and a cigar in one hand. He was said to still be holding the cigar when authorities arrived to examine the body, and his daughter Lizzie's dress was so stained with her father's blood that it would be presented at trial to turn the jury's emotions.

The first man on the scene was said to be Albert Gilchrist, who held Bowman in his arms and swore he would bring his killer to justice. Gilchrist would go on to be governor of Florida and is buried not far from Bowman.

Seeing Bowman's grave in person, you're struck by just how alone he is. While most graves are close together, many with family members, the marshal has no one near him, just a headstone erected by Woodmen of the World and yards of open field. His family was forced to move back to Wauchula after his murder, whether from a lack of money or to get away from the community their fallen hero had not been able to tame.

From stories, it seems Bowman's love for his children and his job might be what keeps him at the cemetery. Many believe the tall man who walks in the section known as Babyland is the old lawman looking after the children. His is one of the closest graves to this area, and he matches the description of the shadowy figure

Marshal John Bowman's grave is set apart from the others.

people see. It works in reverse, as well. People visiting Bowman's marker feel as if they are being watched and hear the children laughing and talking behind them more than at any other location in Indian Springs.

There may be other reasons his spirit cannot find peace. From reports, there was chaos at the time of shooting. Three men were seen fleeing the scene, although dogs were brought in and tracked the killer in a different direction. Two men were eventually identified as Johnnie Matthews and Pope Henderson, who turned on the third man they said was the ringleader. Isaiah Cooper came from out of town and had run-ins with Bowman over his illegal whiskey business. People later testified to hearing him threaten Bowman, although he had an alibi for the night, and no gun was ever positively identified as the murder weapon. Witnesses were brought against Cooper to testify about what a horrible man he was, and even a psychic told the court he had done it. Despite the lack of evidence, he was convicted and sentenced to die.

This should be where the story ends. The problem was that there were too many wheels spinning behind the closed doors of Southwest Florida politics. After spending time in a small cage in the Florida heat, Cooper was shipped off to the then seat of the county, Arcadia. New gallows were built, and people eagerly awaited the day the cop killer would hang. Two hours before he was set to die, the governor granted him a stay of execution for reasons unknown. The crowd was furious and was set to storm the jail and take justice into their own hands, but as they approached the steps, the train whistle went off. They decided to catch the ride home rather than go through with their plot. Cooper was granted another stay, and then in 1909, the new governor commuted the sentence to life in prison as his first act in office. This governor was Albert Gilchrist, who held his friend and told him he would not let his death go unavenged. In 1913, Cooper escaped from a work camp in DeLand when the guard who was watching him refused to follow him into the worksite for fear of dirtying his shoes in the Florida swamp mud. Oddly enough, there is no record of Cooper ever being in the Department of Corrections system. He may not be one of the spirits in Indian Springs, but it seems that in many ways Isaiah Cooper is a ghost of a different kind.

John Bowman has enough to be upset about. He was laid to rest alone after dying a graphic death and having his convicted murderer set free by the man who promised him justice. That should be enough, but there is one more twist to the story. The first man brought in for questioning on his shooting, well before Cooper's name was ever brought up, is laid to rest even

A deadly love triangle? Ma McGraw with her two husbands, Dick Windham and Mac McGraw.

closer to Bowman's grave than Gilchrist. He was a mover and shaker in the political scene of the county at the time and would go on to become the county's first commissioner when Charlotte County broke off from DeSoto County and Punta Gorda was made the county seat. His name is Richard "Dick" Windham, and the marshal might not be the only person he sent to Indian Springs Cemetery.

Only his other victim is buried next to him. In what must be one of the oddest alignments of plots, Dick Windham is buried next to his wife at the time of his death, Virginia "Ma" McGraw. On the other side lies Ma's first husband, George "Mac" McGraw. Rather than being buried on opposite sides with their common wife in the middle, the two men are next to each other. To make matters worse, it is said that Windham was having an affair with Ma at the time of Mac's death. There are many rumors whispered throughout the archives and history books of Charlotte County about the creepy and sketchy nature of Windham, but the one almost everyone agrees with is that Ma and Dick conspired to kill Mac and frame another man for the murder.

By 1931, at the height of Prohibition, Ma and Mac's place had become one of the most successful businesses in town. Business was booming in Punta Gorda as the Atlantic Coast Railway Line, also known as the Acline, established a loading dock for turpentine and lumber. Across from the stop was the McGraws' store, which sold gas, food and candy, but its real business came from illegal moonshine and other spirits. While the official name might have been McGraw's Place, everyone knew it as the Bloody Bucket. How the place got its name is still debated today. Some say the clientele sometimes got too rough, while others say Mac was a bit of a scare himself and was known to knock heads to keep things moving respectfully in his place. More than likely, however, it came from Ma's signature drink. She used the strawberry syrup that was set beside ice cream and other treats and mixed it with equal parts moonshine to create a bloody-looking mixture that went down easy and took you down even easier. She was known to serve the 70-proof concoction to the boys in the town. The truth is that the name probably came from a combination of all three because there were reports that the Bloody Bucket drink had a reputation for causing fights that escalated quickly.

Everyone in town knew Ma and Dick were having an affair, including Mac. It may even be that he looked the other way, knowing the power Windham had in town and how difficult he could make it for the Bloody Bucket if he wanted to. That may have been a fatal flaw for Mac, though. In 1931, the place was robbed by Joseph Hugeen. As Ma looked on, Hugeen shot Mac in the back ten times, although he was still able to get into the back room and get his own rifle and kill the assailant. The only witness who survived was Ma, and only one gun was found after their deaths. Most people in town agreed that Hugeen had been set up by the couple who figured a robbery would be a great way to get rid of their problem.

Windham and McGraw eventually married in 1946. She was out of the business by then, and it had converted to a more respectful establishment after Prohibition, named the Alligator Bar, although she was said to have connections to whiskey and rumrunners from Cuba to the Carolinas. She died in 1948 and Windham in 1953. Could it be George Mac's spirit that wanders the cemetery, trying to get away from the couple who conspired to kill him? Maybe he just can't stand to be so close to his ex-wife and her lover.

Unfortunately, the most likely candidate for the screaming woman might be the saddest story in the graveyard and might not be a woman at all. The cemetery land was donated in 1886 by businessman James Sandlin, who also has the honor of being the first man married in the town. He would need the land himself only a few years later, when he died, possibly of tuberculosis. Of the tragedies his family suffered, the one that has continued to draw the attention of locals and folklorists is that of his daughter Mary Leah. One day, Mary was ironing on the front porch with a kerosene iron, when her dress caught on fire. She ran down the street screaming in pain before people were able to catch her and put it out. She died three hours later and was laid to rest next to her father in Indian Springs. Her story, however, does not end there. One of the most famous haunted buildings is the house she lived in at the time of her death, the Sandlin House, overlooking Charlotte Harbor. For the past one hundred years, her spirit has been said to walk the rooms of the house, and although it has changed hands time and again, Mary has found no peace. She has been seen walking down the halls and hiding in closets. One family who owned the house refused to sleep in the upstairs bedrooms, where her tapping and skipping was so common. Another claimed to have heard her whisper their names. There are also stories of her slamming doors and even a time when she deflected a bullet from a shooter, causing it to come back to him and wound his leg.

With so many stories fueling the legend of Mary Leah, it's not odd that people associate her with a ghost near where she is buried, especially one that screams. Some claim it may be her spirit replaying the moment of her accident over and over, although that seems unusual, given the circumstances. Paranormal authorities will tell you a residual haunting, or an intense moment of death or injury, can play itself over. That usually happens at the spot of the incident—not five miles away where the person is buried. People also question whether a ghost can haunt two different places.

The other candidate for the screaming woman might not be buried in the cemetery at all. In one section of the cemetery, right near where Bowman is buried, there is a section called Babyland. Sectioned off since Hurricane Irma in 2017, it was set aside for those who had died in the county as small children and newborns and whose parents did not have enough money to give them a fancy burial. While some of the markers contain full headstones, others appear makeshift and unattended. While supporters of the cemetery spend time taking care of the markers and graves, some were laid to rest in such a simple way that interfering with the way they look would be going against the historic aspects of the location. An outside theory suggests that

Babyland, the site of ghostly children and their protector.

the screaming woman might be the mother of one of the small children who returns to the cemetery to loudly grieve for her child and mourn the fact that they are not buried together.

Cemeteries are often bad places to get ghost stories. They are cliché and overdone and too perfect of a setting. There are too many reasons to see things, like the moonlight off stone or gas escaping from the ground. They are fun to mention briefly and then move on to one that goes deeper. That can't be said for Indian Springs, though. If the history doesn't scare you, there is always a cast of characters who come out at night and beg to be heard. It is one of those cemeteries that lives up to its reputation; just don't expect to know who the ghost is that's tapping you on the shoulder or whispering your name.

14

THE ASTOR SENTINEL

You've been to Astor, Florida, before, even if you've never been anywhere near it. It's one of those small towns across America that are labelled unincorporated—someplace you pass through without knowing the ZIP code has changed or that you've even entered another county. Part of the town is considered the outskirts of the famously haunted Ocala National Forest, but most don't consider it at all—unless you live there. The residents are walking encyclopedias of its history, as if each has a place on a tourism board that doesn't really exist, and they take great pride in their town, although they are quick to point out that there is something unexplained and odd about the things that happen there. There are mobile homes and sprawling ranches, and people there take things at their own pace. When you pass over the drawbridge that crosses the St. John's River, you're supposed to change your whole mindset. If you ask a local, they say they run on Astor time the same way people on the Keys say island time.

The town may have been born to fail. Depending on how you look at the world, Astor is either the little town that could or the town that was never meant to be. "We push on, but never seem to be able to get out of our own way," says Elise Van Cise, a local librarian who knows the town history well and who has had many of her own paranormal experiences there. "It's like this town has a little foot on it that says, 'You can't do that yet.'"

Born and defended by blood, this small stretch of land is bordered by a swampy river that acts as a roadmap of the haunted and cursed history of that part of Florida and a dark forest that has been a magnet for the

Morrison Island
in Astor, home of
the guardian.

unexplained. Astor has tried to be something more—something like its
neighbor DeLand. For almost five hundred years, it has struggled, but like
Sisyphus rolling the boulder up the hill, it remembers enough about its past
to have pride in where it comes from—but not enough wisdom to learn
from its mistakes. Yet the townspeople also have pride in those mistakes, and
while they joke about the way their town has risen and fallen since it was first
founded, so many of them can recite its history and talk about the characters
who made their way to the town. There's the failed railway and the claim
that it was once the wine capital of Central Florida. There's the building of
the Astor Bridge to connect it to the industry of the surrounding towns and
then the killing of McQueen Johnson—the first man to run it. That case
remains unsolved because the bridge crosses two different counties and no
one wants to claim responsibility for it. There are still airplane bombing tests
on the edge of town in the Ocala Forest.

When you talk to someone from Astor, you realize they have as much pride and interest in the legends of the town as they do its history. They can recite the tale of the Hanged Monk and Oklawahumpka the same way other people can recite their town's Revolutionary War heroes or their town founders. There is a certain amount of pride when they tell you about Pink, their very own version of the Loch Ness Monster. These are not just legends or ghost stories but also part of the structure of the town, passed on and experienced.

The history of the town is a tale created by the killing of those who were there before. Well before the arrival of Europeans, the Native American tribes who made that area home felt something was off, especially on the east side of the river. It is rumored that some buried their dead in mounds there, but there are more records of guides and friends of the settlers warning people to avoid the place altogether. Admiral Jean Ribaut was a French Huguenot who made his way inland to the area in search of a place for his people to escape religious persecution in 1562. Unlike some of their fellow countrymen to the east, they seemed to create a natural balance with the Timucua and lived in relative peace for half a decade. In 1566, this ended with the arrival of the Royal Fleet of Spain. In the next three years, they destroyed all evidence of the French, killing all the settlers and setting up a new Franciscan mission in St. John's name.

The Spanish did not mix well with the Timucua, who swore revenge for the French. They burned the mission and killed all but one of the monks, who they put on trial. The longstanding narrative is that they tortured him before hanging him from a tree. The Spanish then sailed down the river, burning every village and killing any Timucuan they found. Unlike the Huguenots, they did not establish a balance with the land but instead wrote about it being filled with serpents and dragons. Perhaps monsters in the dark are born from always having to look over your shoulder. The Spanish spent the next 150 years fighting Native American tribes and other European settlers to keep the land, until they were eventually forced to give up the area to the English.

It is said that the monk appeared that first night after his death. The legend goes that a boy fishing on the banks of the river saw him first and reported it to the rest of the tribe. They then witnessed a "white and fuzzy" figure walk down the road toward the tree where the monk was hanged. The chief ran to meet him while the rest ran away in fear. The next day, the chief was found dead without a mark on him. Since then, it is said that the monk returns on a full moon around midnight to travel back to the place of his death. Perhaps this is the ghost that is still reported to be seen in the town, especially on Gobbler Road, walking the streets, disrupting the trailers and homes nearby and allowing cars to drive through him. "Late at night, between 11:30 and 1:00," says one local, "you see nothing as you're driving, and all of a sudden, there he is. If you look in your rearview mirror, he's gone." These kinds of encounters are common in the town.

Others say it is actually the spirit of Oklawahumpka. Ghostly legends get mixed and matched in Astor. Even the ghosts are on Astor time. If the monk's story is one of revenge, then Oklawahumpka's is a saga of the love of his people and the land. There are all kinds of stories told about him, and if it is the old Euchee chief, he might not be a ghost at all but a man who has never died.

His name means "the man who cannot die," and he is the last of his tribe left to look after the land. The Spanish came through the area and defeated the tribe but could not kill Oklawahumpka, whose only wound was a lost toe said to be bitten off by an alligator in his youth. The Euchee tribe was not in that part of Florida when the Spanish arrived but joined the Muscogee Creek Nation and moved west to Oklahoma or joined what would become the Seminole tribe in the 1800s. It's impossible to tell if he came from Tennessee to escape when his people fell or whether the Euchees got confused with the Timucua somewhere along the way.

His people and heritage all but wiped out, Oklawahumpka escaped, taking his tribe's burned totem pole from their sacred mound. He made his way to a small island in the St. John's River, which today is called Morrison Island. It is a small inlet in a swampy part of the river that the local tribes took to call the Forbidden Swamp. A few years later, when Don Huertas received a grant for that land, he brought twenty-four soldiers with him to survey the territory. Half went to Morrison Island and were never seen again. The surviving dozen men reported hearing the "piercing cry of some large bird, probably an eagle or a hawk." A hawk was the spirit animal of the Euchee and the primary symbol on the totem Oklawahumpka had brought with him. Over the next few centuries, the man who cannot die has been said to be responsible for the death of pirates who came into the area, soldiers, surveyors, townspeople who did not respect the territory and even Seminole who did not respect the old ways. All the disappearances and deaths have been accompanied by the cry of a hawk.

There have been reports of mysterious footprints in the mud surrounding Morrison Island at times—all said to be missing a toe. These are said to appear all over the western part of Astor, so the glowing figure seen on different streets might be Oklawahumpka and not the monk. The legends say that he was the largest man people had ever seen, and he has been compared to a mountain or a giant bear. While there are plenty of bears in the woods throughout the town, there are also reports of Bigfoot, which may be the last man of the Euchee tribe as well.

People still go missing in the area, and some locals attribute it to the ancient Euchee, and Oklawahumpka has even been linked to people who have been killed in the Ocala Forest. At first glance, it might appear to be the work of a vengeful force, but the real root of the legend is love. Oklawahumpka is trying to protect the last parts of his heritage, and the stories of missing people may be the work of bears and alligators instead of retaliation. Once a legend takes hold in a community, people find it easier to blame the good and the bad on it. If that doesn't convince you that this spirit is one of love and security, then the most widely told tale surrounding him might.

Oklawahumpka stands guard on the island every night. The people of the town will tell you that he is on watch and that this is one legend that is seen by people frequently. People report that a man will suddenly appear on the island at the edge of the water, visible from the Astor side with the best view being from Blair's Jungle Den Fish Camp. He strolls along the water for a bit before walking in. He goes up to his waist, then his neck and then disappears. One woman claimed, "At 11:30, you can see an old Indian walk out from the island out to the water."

A man has also seen someone on guard. "My girlfriend took me out there. I didn't want to leave because I felt something. Something was out there. I was just watching it. It was like it was there and not. And I was just watching it with my mouth open. I had heard of it, but I was seeing it."

Some people are able to make out a figure only, while others see features, but they all describe him as being taller than most men and muscular. Some have even said that he will smile at them and nod, as if telling them to move on. Even those who have not seen him know the story, and it used to be a popular legend trip to go out there at 11:30 p.m. and try to catch a glimpse of him.

Of all the folklore I have tracked down in Florida, this is one of the few I have seen with my own eyes. I went to Astor to speak at the library and was told the story by several of the patrons. We went to the Jungle Den that night a little past 11:30 p.m. because we had been looking into another local legend. As we stood there, intimidated by the obvious sounds of alligators and the not-so-obvious sounds of other wildlife, a solid figure appeared

One of the roads said to be haunted, maybe by Oklawahumpka.

across the water from us. Even though he appeared as only a little more than a shadow, I could tell he was tall and solid, like he was made of wood. He had no shirt and straight dark hair. He glided as he walked, rigid and giving the impression of a soldier during a formal march. I could not see his feet, but he made his way into the water before disappearing behind a tree. I

The Jungle Den is said to be the best place to get a glimpse of Oklawahumpka on Morrison Island.

then heard a splash and could see his head and shoulders floating above the water. The animals around us became almost deafening, like someone was disturbing their territory, and then he was gone.

Like the person who had shared his story at the library, I stood there with my mouth open and listened for any more movement of the water. But it was over, and the animals settled down again. When I retold my story to some of the people from the town, they shrugged instead of being amazed at what happened to me. That's the way ghost stories go when you're on Astor time.

The legends continue to be told there, and it is the not knowing that allows them to be placed into whatever part of history the teller needs. There are plenty of stories to choose from in Astor. It might be a ghostly figure seen on a road as the fog settles in or a mysterious knock on your camper when no one is there. It could be a man who cannot be killed still protecting what little he has. In this small town in Central Florida, there is no difference between a history book and a ghost story. It all depends on the history you're trying to tell.

15

THE LOVE POTION OF LORIDA

The only motivation more powerful than love is desperation. Put in the wrong situation, a good man will do things he would never have contemplated before. Love may lift your heart, but desperation lowers it. Too often, the two play with each other, and those soaring highs of passion can make one sink even deeper when it is not met by another person. Put in a corner, what would you do? What would you do if it was for love?

It's unclear what brought the man to the bridge that night, but it was definitely either love or desperation. He met the old woman by a full moon to purchase a love potion, but we do not know his motivation. There might have been a specific woman he had his eye on or something more economic on his mind. The old woman was well known at that time as someone who was well trained in mixing herbs and conjuring the elements to make things happen. No one uttered the word *witch*. The people in the town were too dependent on her folk remedies and were too used to consulting her to use that word. There was nothing evil in her eyes or suspicious in her actions to warrant the tag that they saw thrown about describing women with stringy hair and long hooked noses. In some parts of the country, that kind of label could get you killed, and she was useful and harmless, if not a bit godless. But that could be overlooked. She was just an old woman who knew things, much like the medicine men of the Seminole who had been on this same land before them.

It's odd that the man didn't ask about the price before he agreed to meet her. It was steep, showing her true intentions. In return for the love potion that would bring his true love into his arms, all he had to do was give her

Arbuckle Bridge in Lorida, home of a love story gone wrong.

his firstborn child. He was infuriated. He grabbed the crone, swearing to anyone who might have heard them on that night that he would not make such a sacrifice. In the struggle, she fell from the bridge and was impaled by a cypress tree growing near the banks of the water. He knew what he had done would condemn him, and he thought nobody would miss the old woman anyway. Weighing the body down with stones, he drifted her out to the middle of the creek and let her drop to the bottom of the swampy water. Then he ran for a new town, never to return. At least that was his intention.

The next part of the story gets hazy. Some say her ghost began to appear on the bridge, pointing to where her body lay on the bottom. Other stories say that by the time the man left town, her body had floated back to the top, revealing his crime. Most of the people who continue to see her don't care which of these stories is true. They just know she is still seen on the bridge, especially during a full moon. It's a story that's been part of Arbuckle Creek long enough to outlast the town itself, and some modern reports say that she may have gotten her revenge in death. There's more than one spirit on the bridge in Lorida, and they may still be playing out a deal gone bad seventy years later.

When I hear a story like this, the first thing I try to do is relate it and see if the story makes sense with the area. Some shout about the way the neighborhood views itself and its invaders or makes sense given the setting.

The docks at Arbuckle Bridge, where the witch and two male figures are seen.

This legend, while familiar in its elements, seems so isolated that there just might be something to it. While I originally discovered the story on Haunted Places, a website dedicated to listing haunted places, there were enough whispers about it and enough odd moments in the history of the town to make it worth exploring.

Lorida is a ghost town, another victim of the train boom and its own geography. There was obviously something odd going on there before it was settled. The Seminoles, trying to make their way south during their early period of migration, suffered major casualties trying to cross the lake nearby. They ended up naming it Lake Istokpoga, which means "lake where someone was killed in the water." The towns grew up around the body of water, and while those who called it home seemed to enjoy the land while they lived there, it rose and fell in less than one hundred years.

The town was first settled in 1910, when people moved in around the bank of the lake. There was plenty of land to graze and open space, so people started to put down roots. The name was changed from Cow House to Sunnyland to the Hamlet of Istokpoga. The name stuck, but when the Acline Railway came through and started a small settlement to coincide with its rail stop on the other side of the water, people began to get confused over which was which, and mail began to get lost. Mary Strokes, who ran the post office at the time, suggested the unusual name "Lorida," and it seemed to be a perfect fit for the odd settlement. The town found its footing in farming and cattle and grew as the trains came through and roads began to be put down. The town itself has never become as popular or populated as some of the ones around it, with Highway 98 being the only way in and out of town.

It's unclear how well the story of the witch is known in the town, and it feels too old to really take place during its timeline. The year 1910 does not really scream witches and superstitions, even in a small town. Rich Newman, in his book *Haunted Bridges: Over 300 of America's Creepiest Crossings*, puts the meeting in 1945, but he is unable to remember when he found that time in his research. The current bridge was built in 1965, and I was unable to find any concrete evidence on when the bridge became concrete. The bridge itself is not high enough to kill an adult who falls from it, and an older bridge would not have been much higher. The cypress tree reference seems like an explanation from someone who told the tale a while ago.

"Wait, she wouldn't have died falling from a bridge that high."

"Well, aw, she actually impaled herself on a tree growing out of the water."

"Okay, that makes sense."

That is the way urban legends evolve.

The legend takes an odd turn, though. According to almost all versions of the story, the witch began to be seen on the bridge not long after her death and plagued the town enough for the residents to try to stop her nightly appearances. A mob formed, traveled to her shack in the swamp and burned it to the ground, hoping that would stop her. It did not work. Several residents of the town say they remember something about an old shack being burned in the town but were too young at the time to remember more details. It just seemed important and something people were talking about. It might be possible that people in the town were focusing their frustration at the failing town on an older legend of a witch in the swamp. By setting the building on fire, they thought they would be getting rid of some negative element responsible for the lean times, and the 1940s date does coincide with a mass of people leaving the town due to World War II.

That would be enough for any small-town ghost story, but there are other retellings that paint a more complex picture of what might be going on there. The woman has been known to mess with people's radios, appear to cars on the bridge and float over the site of her murder in the form of ghost lights. However, there have been two other ghosts seen at the spot. According to a follow-up comment on Haunted Places, and echoed a few other places online, a man and a small boy have also been seen there. These two have been known to duck under the bridge and out of sight and play with the poles of people who try to fish there. Could it be that the murderer did indeed take the potion from the dead woman and use it? It could be that he is paying the price in death and the ghosts are the spirit of him and his firstborn trapped and forced to stay at the bridge until the witch can find her peace. That, at least, is the story some people tell.

There may be elements of this story that echo Rumpelstiltskin more than reality, but it is just specific enough to make it seem real. Bridges are focal points of legends, from every covered bridge in New England to the Headless Horseman of Sleepy Hollow, but there is something different about this one. The story of the love potion also keeps the legend alive, especially when you consider that it is almost always a woman in the story looking to make the purchase. Men are not usually the ones bent on marriage in the stories and are not the ones given the decision to give up one of their children. There has to be something going on, but the legend has been told too long to find the original version. Besides, the people who travel the road are not wondering about it. They have to focus their energies on not hitting the witch when they drive over the bridge.

Most folklore comes from a need. It may be trying to explain something or trying to teach the history or an important moment to the community. There is something you can track, which is why they are so appealing to people. We understand ourselves by understanding the story. At Arbuckle Creek in Lorida, there is no lesson to learn, no message to the town or reflection of community. There's a woman on a bridge and a father and son. There are just a few ghosts and a story told to explain them. If context builds understanding, you won't find it there, and maybe that means the story itself is more truth than tale—that and a twisted love story with an unhappy ending.

16

TOMOKIE'S LOVE STORY

There's a ghost—maybe. Odd things are happening, so people think the place might be haunted. They don't know why, so they find a story that seems to make sense or one that sounds familiar. There are two people driving down the road, and they get into a car accident. The man is ejected from the car and dies on impact, but the woman survives for a while. She can spot her husband, his dead body slumped under the tree nearby, and all night, as she waits for help to come and rescue her, she reaches out to him and calls his name. Now at the spot of the accident, you can see two balls of light hovering. They seem to be trying to get to each other but never can. Sometimes a voice is heard on the wind.

Simple, right?

If believing in ghosts is thinking outside of the box, folklore and urban legends are the box we use to try to make sense of them. In Ormond Beach, Florida, there has been a story playing out for at least one hundred years. Dig a bit deeper, and you'll see the story might go back even further. Ghost stories about odd lights have been plaguing a stretch of road leading to the Tomoka State Park for as long as there has been a road there. The trouble is, the stories don't live in isolation. Every time you try to neatly put them in some kind of box, a detail wiggles out and attaches itself to another story. Then a true historical event sheds a different light on things, making it even harder to tell what might be fact. More importantly, the event confirms that something else is going on—something bigger than a simple haunting or a wayward ghost.

Tomoka State Park, the home of Tomokie.

The story begins with what could be a natural occurrence that has taken on the name the Ormond Ghost Lights. As ghost stories go, this one is pretty straightforward. As you travel from Bulow Creek State Park on Old Dixie Highway to Tomoka State Park, there is a stretch of the road that goes over a bridge. For decades, people saw orbs flying around the sky there at night and wondered what they might be. The activity seemed to reach its peak in the 1950s, when the flight of the lights was so well known that it was part of the town's collective lore.

People driving along the road were treated to a light show. At times, there would be only one. It might fly through the sky or dance around in a circle and come crashing down. More of the stories tell about two lights that seem to be connected to each other. They may hover or crash into each other. There are even reports of them combining into one. Often described as playful or with a mind of their own, the lights have been known to follow drivers, giving off a low hum, and have even caused accidents and deaths. It is well known that you can pull up to the bridge, turn off your lights and enjoy a show.

This is where the stories start to pile up and become connected to a larger picture. There is a story of a lone motorcycle driver who was killed while following the lights. He is now trapped on that stretch of road and appears as a bright orb with a loud motorcycle engine that follows drivers and then disappears. A newlywed couple driving through broke down after seeing the lights. The man left to get help and never returned. The woman followed soon after, and neither was ever seen again. Their spirits remain on the site now, causing other couples to break down.

These stories sound similar to ghost stories told around the country—even just an hour away at Central Florida's Oviedo Lights. They make for some interesting goosebumps, but their similarity to other widely told tales gives them the ring of legend and not legitimacy. Even the idea of soul-collecting lights stretches back centuries. For example, the Wampanoag of New England believe in the idea of *tei-pai-wankas*, or the spirits of the dead seen in the form of balls of light. They believed these lights would kill people or lead to their deaths, and to die in such a way would trap you as a tei-pai-wanka. The same idea is held by Europeans and European settlers, only the lights are called will-o'-the-wisps.

Sightings of the lights die down in the early 1960s, maybe proving why they existed in the first place. According to a park ranger at Tomoka State Park, "As far as I know that [the lights] has been disproven because of the fog and the lights way back then. The bridge used to be lower. The lights would shine across the marsh and the marsh gases would look like ghosts. That's where it came from." In fact, the current bridge was installed in 1961 and changed the angle at which cars approached the woods. This shift caused the lights to disappear, and with them the ghost sightings pretty much ended. They became just a story that locals told.

Simple. Case closed, haunting solved and retired.

It would be easy to dismiss the ghost lights as just being a natural phenomenon with some creepy stories attached to them, but there are so many tales surrounding their backstory and too many stories being told about odd things happening in the forest to just dismiss them.

For a long time, swamp gases, and just about any other gas you can think of, have been the rational explanation for why some ghosts appear. The logic is sound. Think of the number of cemeteries with their decomposing bodies and all of the orbs seen by the living. However, the questions have never really been answered about why they exist in some places and not others, or why different kinds of gases cause different kind of lights. In fact, the explosions of these gases have never really accounted for the movement of the lights either. Why do some seem to dance or follow people or spin around and combine? Why do some seem to have personalities or even consciousness? In cemeteries, a body is said to take several decades at most to decompose and release these gases. How can stories of ghost lights persist over an even longer time or in cemeteries where the bodies are hundreds of years old? To say the convenient, if misunderstood, explanation dispels all of the ghost stories is less logical than to admit some might be spirits.

This is to say nothing of the physics of how a shift in an angle can cause these lights to immediately go away. The headlights reflecting off the gas caused the ghosts. It makes sense on one level, but the argument falls apart when looked at closely. For example, many of the people who observed the orbs said they would turn off their lights to enjoy the show. How, then, are their headlights causing them? How do headlights account for the ones that were higher in the sky?

Then there are the deeper questions—the ones that establish a pattern of the supernatural and unexplained in the area. The Ormond Ghost Lights are just the most popular of the legends. Others date back further and point to the land being rotten somehow, perhaps cursed for some reason.

The Old Dixie Highway, which was originally conceived as a path between Chicago and Miami in 1925, connects two parks with dark pasts. On one end is Tomoka State Park and on the other is Bulow Creek State Park. It's had its own reports of lights and dark figures in the woods and several reports leading to the theory that a Bigfoot or skunk ape lives there. However, what Bulow is really known for is being home of the Fairchild Oak, also known as the Suicide Tree. For more than one hundred years, the tree has been the spot of mysterious deaths and suicides. From the original owner of the land, James Ormond, who was killed by someone he enslaved in 1817 on the property, to the deaths of his son James II, who was found underneath the oak tree in 1829, and Norman Harwood, who was said to have committed suicide by hanging from the tree in 1885,

The Fairchild Oak, also known as the Suicide Tree.

the place is said to be cursed and to draw out the negative side of people who go there. Even today, the lore says that if you sit under the tree, dark thoughts will fill your head and voices will whisper that you should end your own life. Touching the tree even causes physical pain.

Matters do not get any better when you leave the park. The entire area, not just one section near the bridge, has a dark history and modern occurrences. Take the mysterious fog that might have killed dozens of people in the 1950s and 1960s. Around the same time the Ormond Lights were rising in popularity, a mysterious pink fog was known to come in off the Tomoka River. An unusual number of people died in relation to it, and even more went missing to never be seen again. The locals and legends tell that this odd natural episode was given supernatural significance and directly held responsible for a rise of missing person cases at that time. It also explained why there have been reports of people dying there in groups for hundreds of years, including the disappearance of the Timucua, who had established a foothold before European settlement.

There is nothing to back up the specific claims of the pink fog. Research finds that there are no reports of mass disappearances, although bones have been found in the forest sections of Tomoka State Park. No one has been able to date them, and different stories attribute them to Timucua, enslaved people or even modern residents who were said to have gone missing. The bones, in fact, are still being found. The same ranger said discovering them has been a constant at the location for years, even as recently as this century. "We had slave bones washing out to the grounds here about six years ago. Slave girls from the 1700s. Their bodies were washing up on the grounds."

The odd history of the area has to be taken into account. There are shell mounds, which often point to burial and sacred lands. The largest mound is said to house 150 to 200 Timucua. While they were described by the European settlers who landed in East Florida, they were wiped out quickly by their new neighbors, even though other tribes and even Timucua in other areas of Florida survived.

The Europeans who settled that area didn't fare much better. They suffered rises and falls, while people in other parts of the state flourished. Richard Oswald was given twenty thousand acres in what is now the state park to grow rice and indigo. Although those crops were in high demand, the plantation fell apart in less than twenty years. Bulow was once a thriving farm and the crowning jewel of the area but was decimated by strife until it was left in ruins. That area then became the scene of murders, accidents and suicide, leading to the notoriety of the Fairchild Oak.

The grounds where the springs once flowed freely, now teeming with ghosts.

Nothing seems to be able to last there for long. Plantations failed, settlements went up in smoke and business ventures like hotels and attractions never got the momentum they did in other places. Even the notorious Fountain of Youth springs in Tomoka State Park disappeared, until what was once a reflecting pond brought in from people from all around dried up and now has nothing to show for its once-glorious past.

The plantations in this area also saw more uprisings than other parts of the country. In 1819, Captain James Ormond, for whom the area is named, was killed by someone he enslaved. An overseer named Tom Addison was killed by an enslaved person in 1825. The most notorious of these murders is that of Samuel Huey, one of Oswald's first overseers. He was known to be a harsh man and a drunk, as well as the kind of man rumored to be stealing from the boss. According to several sources, Huey died at the hands of the enslaved people under his charge. Some accounts say they killed him directly, while others say he had an accident and fell into the river and, probably drunk, was unable to swim back to the boat or to the shore. The enslaved people stood by and watched him drown.

There are historical records to back up that Huey did in fact die off the coast of what is now the Tomoka State Park. The records don't get into what has happened since then. Huey's ghost is said to haunt the banks of the river in the back of the park. The ranger says people tell him they feel as though they are not alone while fishing or walking the area. Others report getting sick all of a sudden and feeling the need to leave or feeling lightheaded, as if they are drunk. He says it is widely known to be haunted. "At the end of the peninsula there was an overseer who showed up with seventy slaves to clear it. He was so mean to the slaves they revolted against him. They took him down to the end of the peninsula and drowned him. They replaced him with a mulatto overseer and things went on. You can feel the vibe down here at the end."

In fact, the same ranger says the whole place is said to be haunted, and people report an eerie feeling in different spots throughout. These Ormond Lights, while no longer seen on the bridge, are still seen in other places in the woods. Bones and bodies have been found on the grounds, making it hard to determine who the spirits might be. Some people think the ghosts might all come to Tomokie, whose large statue looms in one corner of park near where many of the mysterious lights and figures are seen. While many of the stories told about the hauntings in Ormond Beach are based on destruction and tragedy, Tomokie's is a love story.

The Great Spirit came to earth every night to drink of the water of life from a great cup. It often overflowed or spilled, creating the spring that was said to have healing powers. Tomokie, a Timucua chief and giant even among his people, wanted to have that power and pass it to the woman he loved, Oleeta. Together they would live forever and rule. He stole the cup and drank directly from the waters of life, defiling it and causing war among the people. It is unclear whether this was a civil war or with another tribe, but the stories tell that he became like a superman, able to fight off large numbers of men himself. A great battle raged between the two sides. Oleeta, a woman known as a great warrior, had never been consulted about Tomokie's plan and disagreed with him about stealing the cup. She raised arms against him and shot Tomokie in the heart with a poison arrow, killing him before she was overtaken by his followers and killed herself. The two sides continued to fight, eventually killing each other off. Oleeta is buried near the spring somewhere, while the location of Tomokie's body is unknown. The cup was said to be taken from the spring and is in the possession of a tribe in Florida and held sacred and safe but is unknown to outsiders.

The shore where the ghost of the overseer is often seen.

People attribute the bones and ghosts to this battle. They say the lights are the souls who died in that battle, the pink fog is a revenge on people somehow and the land is cursed because of Tomokie's offense. This story is spread as part of the origin of so much of the darkness in the area. For centuries, Ormond Beach was in the shadow of the chief's sins.

Only it wasn't

Tomokie is not real and never was. Although his broken and vandalized statue stands tall against the setting sun, his story only dates to 1955, when a statue was created by artist Fred Dana Marsh and a false legend was created to commemorate the dedication of the statue and symbolize what many felt was an idealized version of the people who lived there. Although now a popular folktale, the story seems to be repeated, almost word for word, by different sources, and no original source dating before the 1950s exists. The name seems to be a corruption of the word *Timucua*, and the participants act more like early twentieth-century ideas of Native Americans than what they actually thought, believed or practiced.

That's the way it has always been in Ormond Beach. There is something in the woods that can't be explained. There is something in the moon that makes the odd fogs that float in and take the form of monsters and ghosts. The fact that the stories exist, not whether they are true, tells us that there is a need to explain the shadows moving through the trees and the unexplained movements of the water. Since we have been able to record history there, the place has been cursed and the people have had to shelter themselves against a supernatural battery, one that can't be explained but has to be experienced. There is no need to worry about that, though. There is always a new story to make sense of it all.

BIBLIOGRAPHY

Alexander, Eve. "Who Killed Marshall Bowman?" Southwest Florida Walking Tours. January 2019. https://southwestfloridawalkingtours.com.

———. "Why Was McGraw's Place Known as the Bucket of Blood?" Southwest Florida Walking Tours. January 2019. https://southwestfloridawalkingtours.com.

"Are FSU Dorms and Apartments Really Haunted?" Tallahassee Apartments Near FSU. January 30, 2012.

Balzano, Christopher. *Haunted Objects: Stories of Ghosts on Your Shelf*. Iola, WI: Krause Publications, 2012.

Blackwood, Emily. "Tomoka Lights: UFOs or Just Swamp Gas?" *Ormond Beach Observer*, October 17, 2014.

Burge, Laura Hildick. *Singing River Story*. Clearwater, FL: Apeli Publishing, 2005.

Canfield, Nicole. "Is Fort DeSoto Park in Florida Haunted?" Exemplore. January 14, 2014. http://exemplore.com.

Carlson, Charles. *Weird Florida*. New York: Sterling Publishing, 2005.

Cindi. "The Legend of Bloody Bucket Road." *Country Living, Country Skills* (blog). October 13, 2003. http://www.kountrylife.com.

Cool, Kim. *Ghost Stories of Venice*. Venice, FL: Historic Venice Press, 2002.

"Devilish Ghosts Grasp for the Living at Haunted Astor Car Camping Site." *BackPackerVerse* (blog). November 2017. https://backpackerverse.com.

"Don't Get Too Close to the Tomoka Lights." *BackPackerVerse* (blog). March 2018. https://backpackerverse.com.

Duffy, Maggie. "Mini Lights: The Legend Lives." *Tampa Bay Times*, October 30, 2016.

Dummire, Dana E. "For Whom the Bell Tolls (Atop Hulley Tower)." *Stetson Reporter*, February 17, 1973.

Favorite, Merab-Michael. "The Ghosts of Ringling." *Bradenton Times*, October 28, 2012.

Genesis, Rebecca. "Haunted History of Fort DeSoto Park." *Ghostseekers* (blog). May 18, 2017. http://ghostseers.com.

Hentz, Caroline Lee. *Ernest Linwood; or, The Inner Life of the Author*. Philadelphia, PA: T.B. Peterson Publishing, 1869.

Hoes, David. "Bizarre Arcadia." Phantoms and Monsters. October 11, 2012. https://www.phantomsandmonsters.com.

Jefferies, Stuart. "American Freakshow: The Extraordinary Tale of Truevine's Muse Brothers." *Weekly Challenger*, March 23, 2017.

Jenkins, Greg. *Florida's Ghostly Legends and Haunted Folklore: North Florida and St. Augustine*. Sarasota, FL: Pineapple Publishing, 2005.

———. *Florida's Ghostly Legends and Haunted Folklore: South and Central Florida*. Sarasota, FL: Pineapple Publishing, 2013.

Johnson, Pat. "The Oviedo Lights: Can It Kill." *FuTUres*, October 10, 1969.

"Lighthouse and Keeper's Quarters." Visit the Lighthouse and Keeper's Quarters. June 2019. https://www.kwahs.org.

Lisk, Nettie. "Legends of Silver Springs." *Ocala Evening Star*, June 12, 1907.

"The Manatee River's Legend." *Sarasota Herald-Tribune*, January 2004.

McQuaid, Kevin. "A Ghost Story? Art School's Brush with Afterlife." *Sarasota Herald-Tribune*, October 31, 2002.

Milbrook, Trishana. "The Tribe That Vanished in a Pink Fog." *Mythosphere* (blog). July 12, 2014. https://mythospherejourney.wordpress.com.

Miller, William D. *Tampa Triangle Dead Zone*. Tampa, FL: Tampa Triangle Books, 1987.

Muncy, Mark. *Freaky Florida*. Charleston, SC: The History Press, 2018.

Neslon, Roberta C. "Ringling Abounds with Spirited, Spooky Discoveries." Free Republic. October 7, 2004. http://www.freerepublic.com.

Pray, Rusty. "Cemetery's Spirits Lie in Its Stories." *Punta Gorda Sun*, October 26, 2018.

Russell, Nan. "Ghosts Won't Cross Water and the Walls Speak." Manatee County Historical Society. 1983.

Shortuse, Marcy. "Haunted Arcadia." *Gasparilla Island Magazine*, September 2016.

"A Silent Treat: Key West, Yellow Fever, and Union Volunteers, 1861–1862." National Museum of Civil War Medicine. October 22, 2018. http://www.civilwarmed.org.

Smith, Dusty. *Haunted DeLand and the Ghosts of West Volusia County*. Charleston, SC: The History Press, 2008.

Stark, Brandy. "Ft. Desoto." *Urban Legends of Pinellas County* (blog). May 7, 2018. http://urbanlegendsofflorida.homestead.com.

———. "Haunted Mound, Philippe Park." *Urban Legends of Pinellas County* (blog). April 2019. http://urbanlegendsofflorida.homestead.com.

———. "Mini Lights." *Urban Legends of Pinellas County* (blog). April 2017. http://urbanlegendsofflorida.homestead.com.

Warner, Joe G. *The Singing River: A History of the People, Places, and Events Along the Manatee River*. Bradenton, FL: Printing Professionals and Publishers, 1986.

Wass de Czege, Albert. *The History of Astor on the St. John's, Astor Park, and the Surrounding Area*. Astor, FL: Danubian Press, 1982.

Weber, Lucy. "Is There a Ghost on Cawthon Hall?" *Florida Flambeau*, October 20, 1971.

Wilson, Luke. "Murder Mystery in Turn of the Century DeSoto County." *DeSoto County Times*, July 2, 1987.

ABOUT THE AUTHOR

C hristopher Balzano is a writer, researcher, folklorist and current host of the podcast *Tripping on Legends*. He has been documenting the unexplained since 1994 and has been a figure in the paranormal world through his books, articles and work as the director of Massachusetts Paranormal Crossroads and now *Tripping on Legends*.

Balzano is the author of several books about regional hauntings, including *Dark Woods, Cults Crime and the Paranormal in the Freetown State Forest* and *Ghosts of the Bridgewater Triangle*, as well as the collections of true ghost stories *Ghostly Adventures and Haunted Objects: Stories of Ghosts on Your Shelf* and the how-to paranormal books *Picture Yourself Ghost Hunting* and *Picture Yourself Capturing Ghosts on Film*.

He has been a contributor to Jeff Belanger's *Encyclopedia of Haunted Places* and *Weird Massachusetts* and was one of the writers behind *Weird Hauntings*. He has appeared in more than two dozen other books, often called in to offer insight into the paranormal or perspective on a certain case.

He has appeared on radio stations across the country and throughout the internet and has been called on by television shows to comment on ghosts and urban legends, including the British television series *Conversations with a Serial Killer*. He has been a guest on *Coast to Coast* AM and been a consultant on television shows like *Paranormal State* and *Ghost Adventures*. He formerly ran the Paranormal News at Ghostvillage and headed up Ghostvillage for Kids.